Doubts
&
Certainties

NEA
SCHOOL RESTRUCTURING SERIES

Doubts
&
Certainties:
Working Together
to
Restructure Schools

E   D   I   T   O   R

Peter A. Barrett

Robert M. McClure
NEA Mastery In Learning Consortium
NEA National Center for Innovation
Series Editor

nea PROFESSIONAL LIBRARY
National Education Association
Washington, D.C.

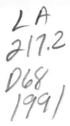

LA
217.2
D68
1991

Note

The opinions expressed in this publication should not be construed as representing the policy or position of the National Education Association. Materials published by the NEA Professional Library are intended to be discussion documents for educators who are concerned with specialized interests of the profession.

Library of Congress Cataloging-in-Publication Data

Doubts & certainties : working together to restructure schools /
    editor, Peter A. Barrett.
        p.   cm.—(NEA school restructuring series)
    Includes bibliographical references.
    ISBN 0–8106–1843–5
    1. Education—United States.   2. School improvement programs—
United States.   3. Schools—United States.   I. Barrett, Peter A.
II. National Education Association of the United States.
III. Series.
LA217.2.D68   1991
370' .973—dc20   90–29158
                                                                    CIP

EDITOR'S ACKNOWLEDGMENTS

Robert M. McClure's foreword, "The NEA Mastery In Learning Project: Individual Growth, Institutional Renewal, School Restructuring," is adapted from his "Individual Growth and Institutional Renewal," which appears elsewhere. Reprinted by permission of the publisher from Lieberman, A., and Miller, L., *Staff Development: New Demands, New Realities, New Perspectives,* 2d Edition. (New York: Teachers College Press, (c) 1991 by Teachers College, Columbia University. All rights reserved.)

A version of Madeleine R. Grumet's chapter, "Dinner at Abigail's," appeared as "Dinner at Abigail's: Nurturing Collaboration" in *NEA Today* 7(6): 20-25.

I wish to acknowledge the contributions of Katherine Epes Barrett, Shari Castle, Shalinda Miles, and Ruth Zimmerman in the preparation of the manuscript.

And I dedicate this book to my daughters, Caitlin and Anna Patricia, who seem convinced that their schools were designed with them in mind. May they continue to find settings in which they can be comfortable without becoming complacent, nurtured without becoming dependent, and sure of themselves without forgetting others.

CONTENTS

Part Three: ROLES

AFTERWORD
Learning Communities:
Reflections on Our Work

Those who will begin with certainties shall end in doubts; but those content to begin with doubts shall end in certainties.

—adapted from Sir Francis Bacon,
The Advancement of Learning

This book is not a restructuring primer, but its organization and its contents do provide different ways of thinking about renewal, with the issue of how to work together toward a shared vision providing a persistent theme. Its purpose is to encourage reflection on your own restructuring plans or experiences in light of these accounts.

EDITOR'S OVERVIEW: WORKING TOGETHER TO RESTRUCTURE SCHOOLS

School restructuring involves the creation of fundamentally new settings that are attentive to the emerging meanings all inhabitants bring to their activities there. Without a renewed sense of community among the actors central to the process—teachers and administrators, students and parents—restructuring will enjoy little success. This notion of community suggests the emergence within particular contexts of new roles and relationships that participants actively shape and take on as they work together to restructure their schools. A collective vision, communication and collaboration, reflection, and ongoing renewal characterize such a community, which shuns the hierarchy, isolation and suspicion, or complacence that often pervades the school.

The participants in NEA's Mastery In Learning Project (MIL), in the project office and at the school sites scattered across the country, have remained keenly aware of the importance of community, not only within individual schools but across schools variously engaged in this process of site-based, faculty-led school improvement. One means of promoting that sense of community was a newsletter, *Doubts & Certainties,* which proclaimed atop each issue (after Sir Francis Bacon's *The Advancement of Learning*), "Those who will begin with certainties shall end in doubts; but those content to begin with doubts shall end in certainties." The newsletter, edited by Dorothy Massie, carried articles of interest to educators involved in school renewal, notes from MIL schools, participants' reflections, and the occasional book review.

MIL national conferences—in Minneapolis, Chicago, and Washington, D.C.—enabled participants to connect names with faces, to celebrate successes and assess apparent failures, and to continue their collective inquiry into school renewal. Some of these participants shared their work with wider audiences at gatherings such as the American Educational Research Association (AERA) annual meeting. And MIL practitioners and researchers forged yet another type of community, an electronic one, through the IBM/NEA School Renewal Network.

Around these publications, events, and activities cluster the tracks of MIL, articles and papers and speeches that do not record merely that project's journey. Instead, they explore concerns that are likely to be central to individuals and schools anywhere engaged in, or intent upon becoming engaged in, such a process. This volume collects some of the writings for which MIL served as the stimulus, the facilitator, the magnet, or the excuse. They are articles from *Doubts & Certainties,* conference speeches, MIL occasional papers, and AERA presentations.

We have relied on three categories—really different ways to think about renewal—to bring shape to the collection: *Visions, Contexts,* and *Roles.* Following MIL Director Robert McClure's introduction to the project and his discussion of participants' experiences building collegiality and using the knowledge base, we consider the conditions that make reform necessary and create a sense of possibilities— visions—for restructured schools. Arthur Costa casts the widest net. His vision of the school as a home for the mind relies on story and metaphor to explore what the school could be and so often is not. He stresses the importance of creativity, deliberation, perseverance, humor, and wonder. Costa portrays school activity as circumscribed by standardized testing, a theme Dorothy Massie extends in the second chapter, which focuses on the need for authentic performance-based assessment that is a productive part of instruction.

The next two chapters, the first on multicultural education and the second on cooperative learning, consider particular strands in envisioned fabrics of schooling. Carlos Cortes sketches out the need for multicultural education in an America in which people "of diverse backgrounds must live and work closer and closer together." A concern for otherness also shapes my piece on developing student voice through cooperative learning, which draws young people into the characteristically human conversation.

Dorothy Massie's chapter on school climate, which taps MIL faculty inventories for ways of improving school settings, closes the *Visions* section and offers a transition to *Contexts*. Here we examine the contexts in which school renewal proceeds, settings that enable and constrain such efforts, and the need to document those efforts. Lynne Miller looks at two quite different restructuring projects that reflect the particular settings in which they emerge, while revealing tensions and barriers common to such efforts anywhere. In similar fashion, Madeleine Grumet's account of a faculty's growing ability to work together in a specific context never loses sight of the larger forces that promote conformity, isolation, and silence. Carol Livingston examines how schools engaged in site-based, faculty-led school renewal can document their efforts in contextually rich ways that inform others and assist participants in the decision-making process. Her work with MIL schools reveals a number of factors that facilitate or inhibit the documentation process. Finally, Shari Castle and her MIL colleagues examine how an electronic community emerged across widely separated contexts through the IBM/NEA School Renewal Network.

The third section, *Roles,* highlights certain individuals within these settings: change facilitators, teachers, students, and parents. Reflecting her belief that "strong adult communities support deeper changes for students," Marylyn Wentworth discusses ways in which change facilitators can help build those communities even in the face of school patterns that can discourage those efforts. The next three chapters—by Gary Rackliffe, Terry Mazany, and Dorothy Massie—explore, in turn, the roles of teacher leader, student, and parent in renewal activity. Rackliffe's chapter relies on the journal of a teacher leader in a school restructuring project, focusing on personal and interpersonal aspects in the context of her formal role. Mazany calls for full partnership for students in school renewal rather than maintaining prevailing approaches that seek merely to control, while Massie similarly urges drawing parents into a sustained, positive involvement in their children's education. Gary Griffin's reflection on the emergence of learning communities through school restructuring picks up many of the themes in earlier chapters, weaves them into an afterword, and closes with a sense of anticipation appropriate to schools and the work of restructuring them.

—Peter A. Barrett, Editor
NEA National Center for Innovation
Washington, D.C.

FOREWORD:
THE NEA MASTERY IN LEARNING PROJECT: INDIVIDUAL GROWTH, INSTITUTIONAL RENEWAL, SCHOOL RESTRUCTURING

by Robert M. McClure

The NEA Mastery In Learning Project, a site-based, faculty-led, school improvement project, completed five years of intensive research and development activity in Spring, 1990. The Project attempted to learn about what happens to educational quality when a school faculty, organized knowledge, and the authority to act are brought together in the school. The following is a brief summary of the effort, its outcomes, and its continuation.

MASTERY IN LEARNING

The project and its successor, the MIL Consortium, share a focus on the essentials of schooling—learning, curriculum, teaching—and how these interrelate to define the culture or climate of the school. Project resources enabled the faculty to create the conditions necessary for students to master important knowledge and skills. MIL asked the faculty and its community to recreate their school to reflect:

- The best that is known about teaching, learning, curriculum, and climate; and

- the faculty's and community's best aspirations for its students.

In other words, the Project did not predetermine what schools should be like as a result of reformation and then set out to achieve that vision. Rather, it set out to test the idea that school faculties with

15

access to current knowledge, research, and exemplars of good practice could, given the authority, "grow a school" that would better serve its students than one reformed by outside mandates.

A NETWORK OF COOPERATING SCHOOLS

Following publication of The National Commission on Excellence in Education's *A Nation at Risk* (1983), many school renewal efforts, particularly those initiated by state legislatures and governors' offices, relied on a mandated, top-down approach to improvement. To demonstrate to policy makers and others the efficacy of another approach, MIL created a demographically representative network of schools. At the outset, six schools were chosen to participate in an 18-month pilot effort. In those schools, the concept of faculty-led school renewal was explored in considerable depth with teachers and principals and other faculty members and with community representatives.

At the completion of the pilot phase, a full-fledged network of 26 schools was formed. Selected from a pool of 1,400 applicants, the schools were chosen using criteria designed to produce demographic representativeness. Upon selection, each school received an invitation to participate in the Project, stipulating that the faculty must vote in excess of 75 percent in a closed ballot to accept the invitation. All of the invited schools exceeded this requirement.

As a group, schools in the network were representative of all schools in the country with regard to socio-economic levels, ethnicity, race, type of community, and nature of the organization of the school. The total student population was 20,280; there were 1,198 teachers; 454 support staff; 64 site-based administrators. The student populations in eight of the schools were racially balanced; in six of the schools, Black, Hispanic, American Indian, and/or Pacific Islanders were in the majority; and in 12 of the schools the student populations were majority Caucasian.

There were 12 different grade-level patterns in the network, including a K-2 and a K-12 school as well as the more usual

16

arrangements. Thirteen of the school were elementary; eight were middle or junior highs; five were high schools. They were in 20 states and in 25 school systems.

Although the local faculty (defined as teachers, administrators, and others at the school responsible for the educational program) designed the reform agenda, the Project provided the processes by which the restructuring occurs:

- *Phase One:* PROFILING THE SCHOOL (several weeks). Through structured interviews with teachers, students, parents, and administrators, a description of the school is created to serve as a benchmark for the Project's efforts.

- *Phase Two:* INVENTORYING THE FACULTY (several days). Through a process that reveals similarities and differences in priorities and aspirations among faculty members, the school faculty establishes initial priorities for improvement.

- *Phase Three:* FACULTY ENABLEMENT (two to three years). The faculty works to create the skills, attitudes, and inclinations necessary for sustained inquiry into the assumptions and practices that define their school.

- *Phase Four:* COMPREHENSIVE CHANGE (ongoing). Having developed skills and habits of collaboration and collegiality and a clearer vision of what is desirable for their school in regard to learning, teaching, curriculum, and school climate, the faculty engages in ongoing systemic school improvement.

As the teachers and administrators talked about curriculum, teaching, learning, and school climate at the outset of the Project, several characteristics emerged:

- Principals and teachers relied heavily on textbook manuals, mandates from outside the school, directives from supervisors, and advice from others in similar roles. They accepted the status quo and doubted that challenges to it would have much impact.

17

- Most of the practitioners in the network knew about or had experienced previous efforts to improve schools and believed that much of that work had been misguided and done more harm than good. They believed that it was their responsibility to resist efforts that would, once again, do damage to educational quality.

- Most staff members did not describe themselves as risk takers. They saw their school systems as closed organizations uninterested in input from "low level" staff, organizations that punished those who took risks.

- School staffs accepted, almost unquestioningly, the technologies that control schooling: behavioral objectives, textbooks, and standardized tests. (McClure 1988)

Analyses of the Faculty Inventory (Phase Two) always revealed a number of problems, unresolved issues, and aspirations. In a typical network school these included:

Problems: several kinds of communication problems, chiefly among staff; physical space; lack of materials; lack of cooperation between board and teachers; lack of community involvement; student placement; lack of follow-up of inservice workshops; and teacher burnout.

Unresolved Issues: ability versus heterogeneous grouping; the nature of the student discipline program; teacher professionalism versus labor/management arrangements; internal versus external control of curriculum; and the nature and source of professional development.

Aspirations: learning environment more closely matched to their students; better balance between student- and teacher-directed instruction; teachers using various teaching methods and styles; teachers, parents, and administrators working as a team.

When asked to select words that described their school, the following were often used: *memory, textbooks, uniform classrooms, separate subjects, broad curriculum, student testing that stresses recall, central decision making, teacher burnout.* In "Dinner at Abigail's: Nurturing Collaboration," Madeline Grumet (1989) (See Chapter 7) describes the experience of one school in the MIL network and comments on how these teachers felt about their situation:

> It is less about being overworked than about feeling responsible for the experience of children and forbidden to shape that experience. It is the frustration of being harassed and hampered by the organization of space and time and materials that are essential to your work without having any say about how these resources that shape schooling are distributed. (Grumet 1989, p.21)

SCHOOL RESTRUCTURING: SELF-RENEWING CENTERS OF INQUIRY

MIL's definition of restructuring was shaped by Ted Sizer when he admonished MIL faculty leaders to "Challenge the regularities. Nothing is beyond questioning. Even those things with which we are most comfortable have got to be, not hyperbolically attacked, just questioned—undefensively" (McClure and Obermeyer 1987, p. 6).

At a faculty retreat of one of the schools in the network, what was to be questioned in the name of restructuring was explored:

> . . . curriculum, behavioral objectives, tests, lectures, chalk boards, ten-month school year, fifty-minute hour, six-period day, faculty meetings, bulletin boards, classrooms, pep rallies, grade levels, inservice, drill, student tracking, bookrooms, playground duty, science labs, workbooks, advisories, homerooms, recess, parent-teacher conferences, detention, study halls, classroom management, assemblies, bells, lesson plans, departments, dittos, hall passes, intercom announcements. . . . These and countless other such topics define the forms of schooling, and they are not sacrosanct! (McClure 1988b)

In MIL schools, restructuring is not seen as having a beginning and an end. Most faculty members see it as an ongoing process of comparing current practice with what is known and what is valued and moving to make the necessary changes. This definition of restructuring is changing the norms in MIL schools: They are becoming, as Robert Schaeffer suggested 25 years ago (1967), self-renewing centers of inquiry.

The building of *collegiality* and the *use of the knowledge base* are critical attributes to significant school improvement. The extent to which school faculties have acquired these attributes predicts the depth, breadth, and success of their efforts to achieve significant improvements in educational quality. The following sections discuss these attributes.

COLLEGIALITY

The Project builds on the principle that every decision about learning and instruction that can be make by a local school faculty should be made by that faculty. (Bentzen 1974; Bentzen et al. 1968; Goodlad 1984; and Sarason 1971). To make sound educational decisions, however, requires a faculty that sees itself as responsible for the school and not just a group of individuals who close the doors of their classrooms and do the best possible job without reference to the total institution. As Madeline Grumet states, "Implicit in the MIL agenda is the assumption that what goes on in the classroom is linked to what goes on in the corridors, the lunchroom, principal's office, the teacher's room, even the buses" (1989, p.20).

Faculty in MIL schools began their participation in the Project with high degrees of sociability. When responding to the question, "What is so wonderful about this school that you wouldn't want it changed?" answers from every faculty said something about their close personal relationships with one another. Probably, their closeness as a group, their camaraderie had something to do with the decision to apply to become an MIL school in the first place.

Later, however, it became clear that these relationships were primarily social and, though school-based, not firmly rooted in the business of schools—learning and teaching and curriculum development. In the Project's early days, new definitions of conduct had to be worked out in the schools. Some faculties were not able to develop

20

new ways of working together, to build collegiality, and some even suffered a diminution of their former sociability.

Individual teachers and administrators have chosen not to accept the responsibilities that came with the new ways of relating to one another and withdrew, or banded with persons of like-thinking to become opponents of the renewal work, or escaped by transferring out of the school. Interestingly, school faculties that describe themselves as successfully engaged in school restructuring handle dissidents differently than do others. They are seen as an important balance to others prone to moving the reform agenda more quickly, and that role is acknowledged and respected. Individual faculty members in MIL schools were, for the most part, able to build upon their social cohesion and become professionally engaged with one another.

The progression to collegiality developed through several stages, with some consistency across the 26 sites (McClure 1988a). At the outset, when informed that their faculty had been invited to participate in the Project, most teachers engaged in *testing* of intent, trying to figure out motives, hidden agendas. The trust level was low. Later, with such questions satisfactorily answered, *exhilaration* set in and there were *commitments made* when the faculty felt they were to be treated as professionals and given the authority needed to improve conditions of learning and teaching. Often individuals emerged as leaders at this time who had not served in such capacities before. This phase generally lasted a few months, during the conduct and implementation of the Faculty Inventory and the initial planning.

A couple of months into the first school year, toward the end of October, most faculties experienced the "Halloween syndrome." This phase of *dispiritedness* came about as the staff began to discover that no one from the outside was going to direct them in this effort, that responsibility for the vision, the work, and the results was theirs. At this point, many dropped out of active participation in the Project, returning to what they knew best, teaching solo in their classroom. Now, as few as 20 per cent of the faculty remained actively committed to the idea of faculty-led school reform.

What occurred next—*regeneration*—appears to have been a critical

21

phase in the life of these 26 reform efforts. In effect, they began the work over again, revisiting the data from the Inventory, getting interested in the change process, learning that there was a body of literature about how to overcome such obstacles (e.g. Miller 1988) (See Chapter 6) and using it. Most faculties then *sought to achieve small successes,* acting on a few simple, straightforward ideas (e.g., rules for student behavior in public areas, barring classroom interruptions for most of each class period, beautifying an area of the campus.) These small, visible, campus-wide successes recaptured the interests of a larger number of faculty and were often used as springboards for more comprehensive outcomes.

As the faculty gained experience and confidence in themselves and became more collegial, three other phases emerged which supported their restructuring efforts. One was the *use of research* (which will be discussed in the next section). Another, with profound impact on drawing the faculty together around professional issues, was experimentation; i.e,. interested persons banding together to test an idea and serve as an "R&D party" for the faculty. Some have improved integration of content by combining subjects not usually taught together (e.g., music and math, art and history), developing a new syllabus, teaching it, and reporting the results to the faculty. Others have worked on scheduling, grouping, "less-is-more" approaches to curriculum, integration of special needs students into the mainstream, new forms of student evaluation, differentiated staffing and teaming, expanding teaching repertoires, new forms of governance, allowing students greater authority, and improved parent involvement programs.

Finally, many school staffs within the Project have moved from separate improvement efforts to *a more comprehensive* approach. They see that the school is a system, that to attend to one aspect of it affects another. Through these phases, strong professional relationships across the faculty have supported these schools' renewal efforts. Leaders in these faculties say that this developing collegiality provides the glue that will maintain their school as a self-renewing center of inquiry.

USING THE KNOWLEDGE BASE

Three rules governed a faculty's initial participation in the Project: Seventy-five percent staff approval; full faculty participation in the Faculty Inventory; and commitment that no decision about a reform initiative would be made without consideration of the options available. This last requirement diminishes the all-too-frequent "bandwagonism" that has characterized so many school improvement efforts in the past. Improvement chosen for implementation can, therefore, be undergirded by evidence of worth. As teachers seek these options through assaying what is available, there is also a strengthening of colleagueship and professionalism.

In "Teachers Using Research: What Does it Mean?" Carol Livingston and Shari Castle (1989) defined the MIL view of the knowledge base as "the full range of knowledge resources available to the profession. These include theoretical, philosophical, empirical, and practical resources" (p.14). They go on to conclude, however, that if the school is to be the center of change, it is inappropriate to conceive of a research utilization paradigm in which the practitioner is solely a user, and the researcher is producer. As Ken Sirotnik and Richard Clark contend:

> We must reexamine the idea of schools as centers of decision making and renewal, or we will find that all our discussions of school-based management will simply propel us further along the path toward unsuccessful efforts at change and renewal. If we don't understand the significance of the school as center of change, we will continue to see it only as the target of change. And we will fail to recognize and tap the reservoir of knowledge and talent that already exists there. (Sirotnik and Clark 1988, p. 664)

To combine the latent desire and need by school people for knowledge to aid school restructuring with the resources generated by the research and development community, the Project created a resource base for its schools. This system, designated TRaK for Teaching Resources and Knowledge, has as its purpose to collect and make available to MIL schools in an accessible, user-friendly form the

23

best that can be taken from research reports, other educational literature, and from the field of practice.

For the most part, however, the initial one-way delivery system was an incomplete solution to the problem of narrowing the gap between practitioners and the knowledge base. Too often, there was not the process expertise in the schools to help people use the material and, of course, the process did not foster the objective of creating healthy interaction between researchers and practitioners.

There were also greatly varying definitions of what constitutes research and its uses. Many teachers thought that access to research would provide them with specific answers to persistent problems and were disappointed when they found ambiguity. Others sought to justify current practice ("Research says. . . .") and were displeased when contradictions occurred.

To use the knowledge base interactively, the schools are now connected with one another through computer technology, the IBM/NEA School Renewal Network (See Chapter 9). In addition to the 26 MIL schools, other participants include the federally funded research and development laboratories, several universities, and schools participating in other site-based renewal projects. The system, designed for interaction around topics germane to school restructuring, was conceptualized primarily by assessing the research and development needs of the MIL faculties and their dialogue around such topics as critical thinking, instructional strategies, at-risk students, authentic student assessment, and parent involvement.

Each of the ten focus topics is facilitated by a researcher and practitioners from two or three network schools. It is anticipated that this technologically supported interaction will have a synergistic effect on the knowledge base underlying teaching, learning, curriculum, and school culture.

As faculties have become more sophisticated in their interactions with research other "uses" of research have come to be important—for contemplation and deliberation (the practitioner as critical adapter); for transformation (research as a stimulus for paradigm shifts); and production (active collaboration among faculty and between practitioners and researchers) (Livingston and Castle 1989).

Charles Thompson (1989), who examined reports of several MIL faculties' efforts to interact with organized knowledge to improve their educational program, commented on the enabling, empowering aspect of this work:

> The revolutions reported in this book are not, however, simple redistributions of power. These revolutions do not so much redistribute power as multiply it. New knowledge . . . emboldens teachers to think, to examine their practice, to believe that they are competent to change existing practice. And there is an almost electric sense of energy release that accompanies this realization, a sense of excitement that raises the energy level throughout each building. (pp. 91-92)

For the most part, faculties in the network schools have changed since the outset of the Project. They are increasingly aware of the knowledge base that undergirds their work and are more likely to consider it useful in solving their problems. They see themselves as powerful shapers of the future of their school; are more collegial and less isolated; more savvy about the politics of school systems; better able to view their school in a comprehensive manner. They are more passionate about the values they hold. They feel more influential in affecting student learning.

REFERENCES

Bentzen, M. M. 1974. *Changing schools: The magic feather principle.* New York: McGraw-Hill.

Bentzen, M. M., et al. 1968. *The principal and the challenge of change.* Los Angeles: Institute for Development of Educational Activities.

Goodlad, J. I. 1984. *A place called school: Prospects for the future.* New York: McGraw-Hill.

Grumet, M. R. 1989 Dinner at Abigail's: Nurturing collaboration. *NEA Today,* 7(6), 20-25.

Livingston, C., and Castle, S. 1989. Teachers using research: What does it mean? In *Teachers and research in action,* ed. C. Livingston and S. Castle, 13-28. Washington, D.C.: National Education Association.

McClure, R., and Obermeyer, G. L. 1987. *Visions of school renewal.* Washington, D.C.: National Education Association.

McClure, R. 1988a. The evolution of shared leadership. *Educational Leadership,* 46(3), 60-62.

McClure, R. 1988b. Restructuring schools: Taking inventory and charting direction. *Doubts & Certainties: Newsletter of the Mastery in Learning Project,* 2(4), 1.

Miller, L. 1988. *Restructuring: How formidable are the barriers?* (MIL Occasional Paper No. 2). Washington, D.C.: National Education Association.

National Commission on Excellence in Education. 1983. *A nation at risk.* Washington, D.C.: The Government Printing Office.

Sarason, S. B. 1971. *The culture of the school and the problem of change.* Boston: Allyn and Bacon.

Schaeffer, R. J. 1967. *The school as a center of inquiry.* New York: Harper and Row.

Sirotnik, K.A., and Clark, R.W. 1988. School-centered decision-making and renewal. *Phi Delta Kappan,* 69, 660-664.

Thompson, C. L. 1989. Knowledge, power, professionalism, and human agency. In *Teachers and research in action,* ed. C. Livingston and S. Castle, 90-96. Washington, D.C.: National Education Association.

Part One:
VISIONS

1. A VISION OF RESTRUCTURED SCHOOLS

by Arthur L. Costa

I plan to start off with a few stories because stories build beautiful metaphors, and metaphors are wonderful because they lead to higher-level thinking. Metaphors cause in the brain what psychologists refer to as "a transderivational search." Now that's kind of a high-falooting term, but a transderivational search is what your mind does when it looks for the similarity of attributes expressed by a metaphor.

A metaphor is an implied comparison, sometimes between two things that are quite dissimilar. Life is a waterfall. The coffee is mud (dishwater?). Notice what happens in your brain. You take the attributes of dishwater or mud and give them to the coffee, and that attention to similarities draws you into a transderivational search. After I share some stories, I would like your brain to engage in a transderivational search to pull them together.

ENVISIONING PERFORMANCE

At a banquet in Dayton, Ohio, I sat next to the chief executive officer of Wright-Patterson Air Force Base. Think about Wright-Patterson Air Force Base: militaristic, kind of conservative, engineering, analytical types. What he told me was truly phenomenal: "You know, periodically I bring in science fiction writers to meet with our aeronautical engineers, because it expands their creativity. We believe that what man can envision, man can create."

He also told me: "Periodically, we bring in kindergartners to meet with the aeronautical engineers." Surprised, I asked, "Why do you do that?" He said, "Well, we give them paints, and they paint pictures of airplanes. The aeronautical engineers meet with the kindergartners

29

and ask, 'Why did you draw the wing like this? Oh, so it can go straight up in the air.' And there they are *taking notes* from the kindergartners." What man can envision, man can create.

The next item is from the 1988 Seoul Olympics. Did you realize that there were more psychologists than physicians at Seoul? The reason is that the athletes are already perfect physically; what gives them the edge is the mental preparation. In order to master the body, you have to master the mind first. Have you golfers read Jack Nicklaus' book, *Golf My Way?* Nicklaus says that before he ever hits the ball, he envisions the trajectory the ball will take; he is doing mental rehearsal.

Before he dives, Olympic diver Greg Louganis stands on the board with his eyes closed. In interviews, he has said he is doing mental rehearsal. Before the performance, he envisions his body moving with style, grace, and precision. That mental visioning prior to performance actually sends impulses to the nerves and musculature, what the athletes call the "carpenter's effect." Envisioning in your head seems to improve performance.

Let me tell you another story. At a banquet in Calgary I sat next to a fellow who introduced himself as the director of staff development for General Motors in Canada. I said, "Oh, I know about General Motors in California. We have a plant in Milpitas where they are building the new Saturn in a joint venture between Toyota and General Motors." He said, "Let me tell you about that plant because I've had a lot to do with it. It was the worst plant in all of the General Motors system. The morale was terrible; the number of recalls was the highest; it was a money loser; the attendance was the poorest. In fact," he said, "we closed the whole plant down, and it was my job to rebuild that plant around a new concept."

When I asked how he did that, he said, "Well, it was very interesting. We learned from the Japanese. What we did was to use a lot of the Japanese techniques—you're familiar with quality circles? What we did was to fire everybody, and then we hired new managers. It was my job to get them to *see* a new plant. What I had them do was envision this new plant, where the workers would be working together in teams, where people would be working with each other, where there would be a lot of interaction between management and the workers on the line, where everybody would have a piece of the action, and where everybody would have an opportunity to make decisions. What I did to create this new plant was to get them to envision this new plant. Today that plant has the best morale; it has the fewest number of recalls; it has the highest attendance; and it is the biggest money producer that GM has in its whole system."

Let me tell you another story—and then I am going to ask you to engage in that transderivational search. Robert Redford had his first directing experience with the movie *Ordinary People*. The story goes that Robert Redford wanted to create a certain mood, a certain image, a feeling at the opening of *Ordinary People*. He gathered his cinematographers, his art directors, and his editors and said, "Now look, what I want is to create a feeling of the fall, of kids going back to school." He played some background music and had everybody close their eyes and envision this scene. In that opening scene, you hear the crackling of the leaves in the streets; you can see the colors, the fall colors; you can feel that little bit of crispness in the air as fall is beginning to set in. As you know, Robert Redford won the Academy Award for *Ordinary People*.

Now, I would like you to go into that transderivational search. I have told you some stories about the military and athletics and industry and Robert Redford. What are the commonalities among all these stories?

"There was an envisioning before they were doing; creating a vision before performance."

"A common vision—not only one person, but people sharing in that vision prior to performance."

"Visualizing success—in other words, the image that was created was not only shared, but was also a positive, successful vision, as well."

"Mind over matter. The brain has the power to create new images and to actually create a destiny for your body, if you will, for your own thinking."

31

"It enables one to extend the possibilities; it's a creative aspect; sort of gets you out of the box."

AN EXAMPLE FROM THE SCHOOLS

One more story, this time from education, about a friend of mine named Aldo who teaches seventh grade in a school district on the south side of San Francisco Bay. Let me give you a little background on Aldo. Although his school is in an urban community, Aldo chooses to live out in the country because he wants his five kids to experience caring for other forms of life. The kids, who have pigs, chickens, and a horse, participate in 4-H projects, for example. So the kids have grown up in this environment where they are dedicated to caring for other life. Aldo's family is interesting. Two of his children are dyslexic and always have had difficulty in school. The oldest, Paul, is about 23 now, and despite this handicap, he has been very successful, saving over $20,000 doing odd jobs. He plans to go into business for himself repairing cars, an area in which he has excelled.

Aldo is a great big fellow, like a big honey bear. When he shakes hands with you, his hand encloses yours, and it gives you a lot of warmth. When you go into Aldo's classroom, you probably won't see him immediately because he spends a lot of time with kids, having an arm around them, counseling them—as you know seventh graders need a lot of help, a lot of counseling. Aldo spends a lot of time before school and after school and sometimes gives up his lunch period to work with these kids on problems they have.

Now, in Aldo's classroom, things are kind of messy. What strikes you is its clutter. Kids have put their papers on the wall, and they are in disarray; here is a salt and flower map; over there is one that is not quite finished; here is a toothpick sculpture in progress. It is a busy, messy place.

Aldo's district has entered a new staff development program, Project Praised. Teachers learn the seven steps of lesson design, six steps of classroom management, and five steps of assertive discipline. Being a very forward-looking district, they have even gone so far as to hire coaches (in California we actually call them mentors). The mentors' job is to go into classrooms and coach the teachers in the use of the seven steps of lesson design, the six steps of classroom management, and the five steps of assertive discipline.

Aldo's principal has some concerns about Aldo. First, Aldo does not turn in records on time very much. They are involved in one of these reading management systems and have identified 29 reading skills for kids. Aldo does not keep those records very well.

When the school district went bankrupt in the wake of Proposition 13, they closed down the school libraries. After firing the librarians, they had nobody to care for the book collection which went into complete disrepair. Aldo, who wants his kids to learn how to read, decided that he would take his students to the public library which was about a 15- or 20-minute walk away. On the way to the library, the kids would talk with each other, look at the birds, and study the dew on the grass, the rock formations, the changing leaves, and so on. Now, Aldo's principal believes that this is *not* time-on-task.

Aldo's principal is also concerned that Aldo is probably not using the seven steps of lesson design, the six steps of classroom management, and the five steps of assertive discipline. As I have talked with Aldo, word has gotten around the district that the real job of these coaches, these mentors, is to coach teachers right out of the district, if they do not use these prescribed steps. And Aldo has told me he is scared. He has been teaching for 21 years, and he says to me, "You know, Art, I'd like to do what they want me to do, but quite frankly, I don't know what it is. It's not my style of teaching, and I don't know how to please them. Frankly, I am a bit concerned about myself and about the other teachers on the staff, because we're not conforming to their ways even though we thought we were."

Would you now go back into a transderivational search one more time? What are the differences that you are finding between Aldo's educational career and developments in industry, athletics, the military, the government, Hollywood?

"In the Aldo situation, the vision is coming from the top down."

33

"Aldo is not a member of the vision-generating process; the vision is external to Aldo."

"There is only one vision, and whose is it? Somebody else's."

"It seems that in the first four cases, there was a problem and a solution was being sought; in the last case, they had a solution and were trying to find a problem to fit it."

In *Global Mind Change,* Willis Harman (1989) wrote, "By deliberately changing their internal image of reality, people are changing their world." That is our concern in education. As we envision a new school for the 90's and the decades beyond, we are actually creating a new reality for what is going to happen.

ALIGNING COMPONENTS OF THE CURRICULUM

I would like to share a short course in curriculum development and revisit it several times during this presentation. A critical element of curriculum development is stating goals and purposes—deciding what education is about. A second step is to decide how to deliver the curriculum—what are the methods of instruction, how do we organize schools, how do we select books and develop materials and create the conditions for instruction to achieve those goals.

The third important component of curriculum is gathering evidence to know that as a result of this delivery, we are achieving those goals.

The three pieces are the intention, the delivery system, and the assessment, and they should be in alignment with each other.

As we look toward the future, some of our traditional ways may not work, because if we change our goals, we must also change our delivery system and change our assessment procedure to match them and bring about alignment.

I plan to review with you some of the school effectiveness research of the 80's, see how that has brought about school reform, and consider some of the inadequacies of that research. Then, I would like to look to the future by thinking with you about schools for the 90's and beyond, and to share an agenda for action to bring about that new school for the 90's.

ASSUMPTIONS OF EFFECTIVE SCHOOLS RESEARCH

Effective schools research found—at least it was based upon the assumption—that good schools are high-achieving schools. How do you know if your school is effective? Right—by high test scores; that's number one. We have made the assumption that good schools are high achieving and have high scores.

We have also made the assumption that more content, introduced sooner and taught for longer periods of time, is better. Therefore, we have done such things as flash cards in the crib. How many of you in the past five years or so have actually extended your school year? How many of you have lengthened the school day? How many of you have added more periods to the high school? Those changes stem from the assumption that more of the same for longer time is better.

Another assumption is that external criteria for school effectiveness are valid and helpful for staff change and improvement: "All right, here is a set of criteria identified by effective schools research, and if you'll just do those things in your school, yours will be a good school, too." We've gone through a time in which the criteria have been imposed upon schools, and if you live up to these, if you change yourself, then you will be a good school, too. The criteria have come from outside.

We have also acted on the assumption that teacher evaluation and accountability improve instruction. This is interesting because we have thought that more of the same is better. In ongoing, informal discussions with administrators, Thomas Sergiovanni of Trinity University has asked them what they thought of their teacher evaluation practices. To a person, they said, "They are awful; they are terrible; they don't do any good at all; I hate to do them; I resist them at all costs." When he asked them what they thought they ought to do about that, to a person their response was, "Do more of it. Do more of it." Somehow we have this notion that if we have more teachers accountable and evaluate them more, they are going to change their practices.

Another assumption is that this beautiful, creative act of teaching could be task-analyzed into a recipe. We have broken down this thing that we call teaching into a series of steps and competencies. I know one state in which administrators are trained to go into a classroom with a computer form; they bubble in the Scantron form every time they see the teacher perform one of 65 acceptable state competencies. Further, the administrator is not allowed to confer with the teacher until after the Scantron form has been read by the computer and the data fed out. If you are trying to task-analyze your teaching into a recipe, I would suggest that teaching by the numbers is just about as creative as painting by the numbers.

Another basic assumption is that states can mandate top-down laws and rules to improve education. In many states we find that the states mandate what kind of changes shall be implemented at the local school district, all in an effort to bring about the reforms.

Administrators have assumed the role then that they have to hold teachers accountable and fix teachers. "That's my role, to go in and fix you, if you're not using the acceptable steps and competencies that the state or the district has adopted." Based upon these assumptions, states are making the decisions about the goals, the framework, and the assessment. They look upon excellence as the accomplishment of certain kinds of criteria and attributes, rather than a process that people go through.

EFFECTS OF THE URGE TO QUANTIFY

Now we are being driven by test scores. We are traveling under the delusion that when you cannot measure it, when you cannot express it in numbers, your knowledge is of a meager and unsatisfactory kind. As a result, we find that our schools are trying to measure everything: the amount of time-on-task, the number of questions teachers ask at particular levels of Bloom's Taxonomy, the scores on achievement tests, class sizes, the number of kids, the length of time in school, IQ scores as a basis for grouping, achievement test scores as a basis for excellence, numbers of days in attendance, the minutes of instruction, the percentages of objectives attained, the number of competencies.

Tests have so much influence now on what happens in schools. What is inspected is what is expected. For example, one day at home I discovered my wife's guitar, which she usually keeps at school. When I asked why it was at home, she said, "I'm not going to teach music this year." I said, "You're not going to teach music this year?" "No," she said. Now, in California, in the fifth grade, we teach Westward Movement, and my wife delights in Al Lomax and all the songs of the new frontier, and all that kind of thing. I said, "You're not going to teach music?" And she said, "Nope." "How come?" "Because my kids are not being tested on music; they are being tested in language, math, and reading." What is inspected is often what is expected.

Some people even resist standardized tests. In a school district that gives a pre-test in September and a post-test in June, a primary teacher said to me, "Test scores? Piece of cake. I'll tell you what I do. I give the test in September. I give it late in the day, and I tell those kids, 'You sit down, you're going to take a test, and you're not going home until you've finished.' Throughout the year, we practice bubbling in those Scantron forms, so kids know how to do that. I know what's on the test; it's not like I teach to the test." But she said, "For example, one test item says that Mr. Smith is a used car salesman and has 18 cars on the lot, he has sold five, how many did he have altogether. What I do is take the kids down to the used car lot, and they talk to the man about buying and selling cars so they have that concept, and it becomes familiar to them. Then in June, when we give the post-test, I give it in the morning; I have a party; I give each child four ounces of orange juice to get the blood sugar going; I don't have to worry about test scores at all."

We have been so driven by test scores that we have learned to subvert them and, unfortunately, most of our practices are based upon helping those test scores. We know, however, that those tests do not appeal to the variety of modalities that kids have. We know that those tests give you only a narrow picture of what that kid does at that particular time and on that particular day of his life.

In another school district that does a lot of busing because it is rural, the strangest thing happens. The kids who are poor performers on tests miss the bus on test day, and the test scores seem to go up. But things are changing.

In California's state university system, for example, SAT's and GRE's represent only a small portion of the total number of points you can accumulate for entrance. You are more likely to get into our university system based upon teacher referral, over-achievement, participation in student councils, and activities. Grade point average, drive, achievement, and motivation will probably get you into the university a lot sooner than high scores on the SAT. So we're seeing change.

FROM CONTROLLING TO ENABLING

We are finding that when you *can* measure, when you can express it in numbers, your knowledge is still of a meager and unsatisfactory kind. We have found that we spent a lot of time evaluating how well we have taught what is not worth learning. As a matter of fact, we have found that what was educationally significant and difficult to measure was replaced by what was insignificant and easy to measure. We are having a kind of paradigm shift, if you will, a quiet revolution taking place. We are finding that team building is secondary to the development of the individual, each person in the process. Management is heading for a new state of mind, a new perception of its role and the role of the organization. It is slowly moving from exerting power, to empowering others; from controlling people, to enabling them to be creative. Developing the creativity of the individual is the organization's concern. There is new emphasis on looking at the potential for each person in the process to become more empowered and more creative.

The Greeks had a word for this a long time ago, and they even knew about it before Adler did. The word is "Paideia." The meaning of Paideia is having every quarter of the society contribute to the fullest development of every member of that society. All of our institutions have as a major goal the development of the creative and intellectual potential of every member of that society.

We are beginning to take a different look at schools. Every section of the school would be intent on enhancing the fullest development of the creative and intellectual potential of all of the members of that society. In other words, we are moving away from just the quantitative to look at the qualitative. For example, how relevant is the learning of kids, not just how much time do they spend on tasks? How does a student behave when he or she does not know? Less important is how much students know; more important is how they behave when they do not know the answer. Do they persevere? Do they ask good questions? Are they able to generate creative ideas? Most intelligent behaviors emerge not in terms of how many answers you know, but how you behave when you do not know.

How about using all the senses? You already know that the maximum use of the senses engages all learning. How about learning that is involved with the emotions? We already recognize that learning is memorable, not memorized.

I could tell you to this day with the greatest precision exactly the conditions in which my mother passed away. I can remember walking into that room; I can remember the colors; I can remember the light coming through the blinds. I remember with great precision what I said to my brother when I saw him, and I realized what had happened. I can give that to you verbatim, and you know something, there was no drill and practice; I didn't have any worksheets on it. The emotional overtones enable me to remember it to this day with great clarity. What makes learning memorable is not the number of competencies the kids can perform, but the amount of emotion the kids bring to that situation.

We are looking toward a new goal. We are looking at a whole new kind of organization with a deep sense of purposefulness and a vision of the future, something Aldo lacked, but that General Motors has, a vision of what it can become.

There is a shared sense of ownership and an *internal* responsibility for performance. In other words, I do what I do not because somebody is going to check up on me, not because somebody is going to hold me accountable, but because I feel a sense of obligation to the achievement of that vision, along with my colleagues. I am a member of that team, and I share that common vision, so I am internally motivated, nobody has to fix me, nobody has to check up on me, because I am motivatd internally to achieve. Finally, the environment emphasizes the growth and empowerment of the individual. The environment helps me grow professionally and intellectually. And it is taking place on a local level, rather than being mandated from above.

SCHOOL AS A HOME FOR THE MIND

We are looking foward to a time, then, when the school is a home for the mind, not only for kids, but for all members of that society. Everybody in the school gets his or her intellect empowered; everybody gets his intellect developed. The school is a home for the mind for all who dwell there.

Let me tell you about a principal in California who is working to make her school a home for the mind. She hired a new custodian recently. On his first day, he cleaned a classroom, and then he came to her and said, "Mrs. Zimmerman, would you come look at Room 14, please." So Diane went to his room, looked at it, and said, "Yes, John, this is fine." She went back to her office; he cleaned Room 15; he reappeared in Diane's office and said, "Mrs. Zimmerman, would you come down and look at Room 15?" Well, as you probably know, principals just do not have time to do that. So she thought to herself, all right, school is a home for the mind. What am I going to do? What she decided was to create in John's head an image of the perfectly clean classroom. She worked with him until he had that image. He then was internally responsible to take care of it himself. You see, he did not need her to get the approval because he had that image in his head.

40

One day I went to see Diane, who was busy with another person in her office. The school secretary invited me to have a seat, and there were two little boys sitting next to me. They had been sent to the principal for some disciplining or something. I could not help but overhear these two little boys talking with each other, and one kid said, "You ever been to her office before?" He said, "Yeah." "What does she do to you?" The little kid answered, "She sucks answers right out of you."

As we think about this school of the next decade, of the next century, what does it look like? I have an hypothesis: Teachers will more likely teach for thinking if they are in an intellectually stimulating environment themselves. So one of those curriculum realignments to create is a school in which everybody is going to be developed intellectually; where the school itself is a mediating environment so that everybody gets his intellect developed. What is that going to look like? Let me share with you a few of the principles.

NEW GOALS FOR RESTRUCTURED SCHOOLS

First, I would suggest a new set of goals, not just content goals, but process goals as well. I would want *all* human beings in that school environment to develop some of these intellectual goals. Perseverance, for example. Think about your kids as they are working. Do you ever see them give up easily? Do you ever see your kids crumple their paper, throw it away, and say, "I can't do this"? Do your kids ever say to you, "I don't do thinking." I want kids to persevere, to "stick to it." One of the grand goals of education is to teach kids perseverance, not just how to multiply, but how to behave when they do not know how to multiply.

Do you ever have a situation in which you start to ask a question, and before you even finish, hands go up, and students blurt out answers? Instead of being impulsive, kids should learn to be more deliberative, more thoughtful, to say, "Wait a minute. Let me think about it. Let me process this idea." They can have a plan of action and be more deliberative and more thoughtful in their responses.

41

I want kids to draw on past information and knowledge. Did you ever have a situation in which you say to kids, "Today, class, we're going to have another problem in mathematics, and it's just like the problem we had yesterday. Who remembers how we solved the problem yesterday?" And the kids say, "What problem yesterday?" They say, "Yesterday? I'm not on yesterday anymore, I'm on today now." Kids tend to compartmentalize their thinking into separate and discrete episodes, rather than going back in their knowledge and looking for similarities: "What is this similar to? What does it remind me of? What do I already know about this?" Going back into knowledge is one way that intelligent people solve problems; it draws on past information.

I want kids to know how to solve problems not only independently, but collaboratively, as well. You know one of the great skills of the future is going to be learning how to work together in groups. If you take a look at that General Motors plant, you will not see an individual dropping in radiators or installing hubcaps all day. Computers and robots handle those tasks. Instead, you will see groups of people working together as members of the team. What leaders in industry try to tell us is that in order to work together, you have to be alert to problems and be able to solve those problems as a member of the group.

We want people to be able to learn to listen to each other with understanding and empathy. Listening is one of the highest forms of intelligent behavior. Empathy means the ability to get into the shoes of the other person, to walk in their moccasins for a period of time, what Piaget calls overcoming egocentrism; being able to look at a situation from multiple perspectives, looking at it from many different points of view. You know the main reason why people lose their jobs? They cannot get along with each other. Empathy, communication, cooperation are going to be the great skills of the future.

As I mentioned earlier, the big companies are now valuing insight and creativity in their workers. Therefore, the institution has to focus on and develop the creativity of all people. Now sometimes you hear kids say, "I'm not creative. No, I can't draw. I can't paint." You hear people say, "My Aunt Tillie is good at that. She's good, but it runs on her side of the family." We have a tendency to think that creativity is in the genes and chromosomes, but everybody can develop his creative potential. The institution has a stake in helping everybody realize and develop their potential.

Without a sense of humor, you cannot get along in life. Kids laugh at all the wrong things. As a matter of fact, as you watch television, there is little opportunity to analyze absurdity or satire or irony; instead, the canned laughter tells you when things are funny, rather than allowing you to decide for yourself whether things are funny. So developing a sense of humor ought to be an important goal in education.

WONDERING AND QUESTIONING

We must develop the ability to find the environment awesome and curious. It is wonderful to see kids staring at a beautiful sunset, charmed by the opening of a bud, or fascinated by the geometrics of the spider web. Sometimes we have kids who say, "Who cares? It's boring. That's dumb." I want kids to be turned on and curious. Socrates said that all thinking begins with wondering.

I want kids to learn how to ask questions. Sometimes we conclude a unit by saying, "What did you learn from this?" Did you ever conclude a unit by saying, "What good questions are you asking?" Let me tell you a story about a scientist and Nobel Prize laureate named Isadore Rabi. He tells the story about how he grew up in a Jewish ghetto in New York. When other kids came home from school, their mothers would ask, "What did you learn in school today?" Isadore's mother would ask him something different: "Izzy, what good questions did you ask today?" Rabi says the reason he became a scientist, and the reason he won the Nobel Prize, is that his home valued questioning more than just knowing answers.

We have some new goals. What might a new curriculum look like for the 90's and beyond? First, differentiated and developmental: we know that kids learn differently; we know that kids at different levels learn differently. Probably one of the greatest mistakes we make in education is introducing learning in a symbolic, abstract form, rather than with real, material objects. Piaget called our attention to that a long time ago. Teachers in the primary grades know that kids learn best through experience, through manipulation, through actual participation. It is unfortunate when we forget that principle, and we start introducing reading or math sooner, faster, using symbolic rather than real, material objects.

Boys, more often than girls, populate remedial reading programs in schools. The explanation is that little boys' brain cells mature two years developmentally behind little girls'. We know that the brain cells get a myelin sheath that covers them. Boys get that myelin sheath two years after girls do, so some of their brain cells are not developed fully, yet we start boys and girls reading formally at the same time.

We want all learners thinking. Sometimes we think that thinking skills are just for the gifted. I go to some schools, and I find thinking skills programs have been allocated to the gifted. All kids need to learn how to think. As a matter of fact, we have a new theory in education, that *all of us* are gifted and *all of us* are retarded at the same time. Could that be? Could you be both gifted and retarded at the same time? How many of you never took another math class after high school? Does that mean you are retarded? No, that means you have just one area that has not been thoroughly developed.

How could we reorganize the school to make this happen? First, if we were to believe that school is a home for the mind, then all of its inhabitants' minds would be developed. Everybody in the whole school will continue to grow and learn.

We are going to have maximum caring for the professional staff. We really do not take very good care of our staff in education, I am sorry to say. Industry is different. My daughter just got a new job. She works in an industrial park. My daughter has a small baby. In the middle of the industrial park is a childcare center, because industry is realizing that when parents do not have to worry about their kids, and when they can go to the center for lunch and check and see what is happening, they work more effectively. We have not done that yet; we have a long way to go in education to take care of our professional staff.

NEW ROLES FOR TEACHERS
TO RENEW SCHOOLS

We are going to see some restructured teacher roles and competencies, teacher as researcher, teacher as a mediator of kids' learning. Instead of having tests for political purposes that are advertised in the newspaper, test scores and data are going to come back to the staff to make decisions about curriculum and instruction. Right now, most of our testing and accountability is for political purposes, rather than for instructional purposes. We advertise tests in the newspaper to satisfy the public, rather than to help the professional staff.

Teachers are going to be contributors to the profession. As I look at some of the action research that teachers are producing, teachers are indeed contributors to the profession—a role that we thought the people at the university assumed. But the teacher, who is going to become a new professional, is assuming that role.

We are also going to see teaching of colleagues. We are going to spend maximum time, restructured time, in peer coaching, in teaching each other, in research together, in child study together. The role of the teacher is not one that is confined to the classroom. We are probably the most isolated profession that exists. A lawyer performs in front of the jury. Physicians operate in front of other physicians and anesthesiologists and nurses. We go into our classrooms and close our doors and nobody else sees us perform our beautiful and creative act.

We are going to see an alignment of educational and political views of excellence. For a long time, the politicians and the legislators said what schools ought to be without taking into account the educational principles with which we are operating. They are not looking at how kids learn. They think they can mandate, rather than deal with human beings in the process.

There will come a time very soon when the legislators, the

governors particularly, will turn to educators to say, "What do you mean by excellence?" I feel an alignment coming very soon. We're going to be working even more closely with the politicians and the legislators to bring about laws and funding that are consistent and aligned with educational theory and educational practice.

We are going to see a much closer working relationship with the community, as well. Some of the problems facing education cannot be solved by educators alone. We think about drugs, gangs, homelessness. Do you realize how many kids are homeless, who do not have an address, in our country? That is not only an educational problem; that's a community problem. Working together with human resource development personnel, with law enforcement groups, with social agencies is going to be an important new role in education.

We are not talking about a school that is merely achieving a standard of excellence, but about K.I.S. schools. K.I.S. is a *Keeps Improving School,* because we know that excellence is not a state to be achieved, but a process that we go through, a continuing process. Excellent schools are ones that are continuing to improve, not that have achieved somebody else's standards.

MODELING INTELLIGENT BEHAVIORS

One final condition: Modeling. Ralph Waldo Emerson (1883, p. 95) said, "What you *are* . . . thunders so that I cannot hear what you say to the contrary." If we want our kids to achieve those new goals in the future—perseverance, persistence, overcoming impulsivity, creativity, asking questions—the instructional staff, who serve as models for those youngsters, must behave that way. We know that learning is done best by imitation and emulation of others. If you want kids to listen to each other, you must listen to them. If you want kids to reduce their impulsivity, when there is a crisis in your class or in your school, they have to see you modeling your own restraint. If you want kids to be creative and enthusiastic, you must show them your creativity and enthusiasm.

We do things in schools that really tell kids to do as I say, not as I do. When my wife, a fifth-grade teacher, came home from school upset one day, I asked, "What's the matter?" She said, "Today, I introduced my unit on good nutrition—basic health, diet, good nutrition. Today, in school, we started a candy sale." I know a vice-principal in California who had a very interesting practice, swatting kids for hitting each other. The high school where my daughters graduated had an interesting policy, suspending kids for truancy. You have to walk like you talk; you have to believe so much that all of the behaviors in the school are modeling the development of the intellect, of creativity.

In the school, everybody's mind gets developed, and that means that we as significant adults are modeling those same kinds of behaviors, because the school indeed is a home for the mind where everybody strives to behave intelligently.

REFERENCES

Emerson, R. W. 1883. Social aims. *Letters and social aims.* (Standard Library Edition, *The works of Ralph Waldo Emerson,* v. VIII), 70–105. Boston: Houghton, Mifflin and Co.

Harman, W.W. 1988. *Global mind change: The promise of the last years of the twentieth century.* Indianapolis: Knowledge Systems.

2. WHAT DID YOU LEARN IN SCHOOL TODAY?: IS THERE LIFE AFTER STANDARDIZED TESTING?

by Dorothy C. Massie

If schools were factories, and students were widgets, or cars, or computers, the task of school product evaluation would be a fairly simple one. The analogy, of course, is absurd. Schooling involves the enormously complicated interactive processes of teaching and learning, and students, in their infinite, unpredictable variety, are not products. Most prevailing methods of student testing merely treat them as if they were.

At the very time when the schools are being pressured (rightly so) to teach higher-order thinking skills—the ability to analyze, reason, synthesize and apply knowledge in creative, problem-solving ways—the standardized tests that most students are required to take not only fail to measure those skills, but may actually impede their development.

George Madaus speaks of the "psychometric imperialism" of measurement-driven instruction, which he charges:

> invariably leads to cramming, narrows the curriculum, concentrates attention on those skills most amenable to testing (and today this means skills amenable to the multiple-choice format), constrains the creativity and spontaneity of teachers and students, and finally demeans the professional judgment of teachers. (Madaus 1988, p. 85)

TESTING AND ACCOUNTABILITY

The various educational reforms of the 1980's have brought with them a rising tide of political pressure for school accountability. In the public mind, accountability is equated with standardized testing.

Hence, test scores increasingly have come to dominate the educational landscape.

Test outcomes are critically important for the schools and educators whose performances and reputations are rated by the rankings of their students. And for the students, tests are gatekeepers, conferring or denying status as students move through the schools and into the workplace.

Considering the high-stakes nature of standardized testing today, it is not surprising that many districts encourage teachers to tailor their curriculum to the quick-answer, basic skills content of the tests. It is less defensible, but also not surprising, that some school districts exclude from the tests those students whom they fear will lower their test ranking. Whether or not such tactics actually result in score inflation, they produce nothing in terms of real student achievement gains. The boosting of test scores by another more educationally constructive strategy—reserving class time for instruction in test-taking skills—still does not produce a true measure of students' academic progress.

As the education reform movement evolves, however, demands for accountability are converging on the standardized tests themselves. The tests have become a center of controversy, not only because they fail to measure critical thinking, creativity, reasoning, and problem-solving skills, but also because—largely as a result of the score-inflating tactics described above—their statistical validity is in serious question.

Some leaders of the billion-dollar testing industry, under increasing pressure from education researchers and practitioners, are beginning to work with education reform groups in the search for a better answer to the question of student achievement monitoring than is offered by their current product.

THE PURPOSES OF ASSESSMENT

The question, of course, is not whether to test or not to test. Assessment is intrinsic to the educational process. It is something teachers do every day as they interact with students, assign and grade themes and projects, administer quizzes, interview parents, and constantly observe and evaluate students' performance, their use of instructional materials, and their interaction with each other.

As educators we want students to do far more than just restate facts we have taught them. Our goal is to teach students to use the information at their disposal. We want them to think. Very simply, we're doomed to fall far short of this goal if we are unable to monitor development and measure student mastery of the thinking skills we seek to impart. If we cannot measure the extent to which a skill has been mastered, we cannot determine what to teach next. If we cannot measure the skills we teach, we cannot know if instruction is effective. (Stiggins, Rubel, and Quelmalz 1988, p. 5)

Measurement of students' skills, through some kind of systematic assessment, also has a valid political purpose. The public, whose taxes support the schools, has a legitimate interest in knowing whether students are learning—in determining that a high school diploma really provides some assurance of literacy, numeracy, and the ability to function as a reasonable, responsible adult citizen.

How then can assessment methods be changed so that the effort to serve public information needs no longer impedes, but rather promotes, instructional purposes?

What can be done to ensure that testing will no longer intrude on the educational day, but will be a productive part of it?

What kind of assessment system can be devised that will convey to teachers, students, parents, and policymakers, with validity, more than a one-dimensional picture of instructional outcomes?

LINKING ASSESSMENT TO INSTRUCTION

If progress is to be made toward solving the problems of testing today, it is probably necessary first to recognize that the teaching profession's student assessment record has not itself always deserved high marks.

Education consultant Grant Wiggins (1989b) reminds us that the failure of administrators and teachers over the years to set clear and consistent criteria for student performance has been a contributing factor to the over-reliance on standardized tests, now so educationally intrusive.

If the concepts of shared leadership and school-based decision-making are to be finally and fully an educational reality, then teachers and administrators are going to have to work together to establish consistent and reliable criteria for evaluation, and to develop—or more fully authenticate—performance-based assessment methods that will be a productive part of instruction and will engage youngsters actively in their own evaluation, in showing what they have learned.

Wiggins, who has been a consultant with the Coalition for Essential Schools, describes performance-based assessment in a manner that gives new meaning to the term, "teaching to the test."

> Do we judge our students to be deficient in writing, speaking, listening, artistic creation, research, thoughtful analysis, problem-posing, and problem-solving? Let the tests ask them to write, speak, listen, create, do original research, analyze, pose, and solve problems.
>
> Rather than seeing 'tests' as only after-the-fact devices for checking up on what students have learned, tests should be seen as instructional, the central vehicle for clarifying and setting intellectual standards. The recital, debate, play or game (and the criteria by which they are judged), the 'performance' is not a check-up, it is the heart of the matter, all coaches happily teach to it. (Wiggins 1989b, p. 41-42)

It is a message that makes uncommonly good sense: Make sure the tests have educational validity, that they focus on valued skills and understandings, and the tests will promote instructional goals, they will be worthy of "teaching to." As Wiggins (1989a) commented in an interview, "Let's reverse priorities. Let's honor assessment in teaching and learning and then make that system of assessment more rigorous, more authentic, and more acceptable to policymakers."

In *Dimensions of Thinking,* the Association for Supervision and

Curriculum Development stresses the interrelatedness of sound assessment and instruction:

> Good assessments are more similar to than different from good instructional tasks. Both use rich, sustained, and complex tasks to provide opportunities for the desired thinking skills and dispositions to surface. Both articulate the criteria for effective performance and give students meaningful feedback. (Marzano et al 1988, p. 141)

Teachers are already engaged in this kind of performance-based assessment throughout the school term or year when they evaluate materials students produce. Included are writings and drawings, journals and notebooks; oral presentations; debates; spelling bees; role playing to demonstrate students' grasp of concepts and value considerations; extended assignments such as oral history projects, interviewing and profiling community leaders, organizations, or businesses; projects in science, history, literature, journalism, theater arts; and portfolios of student works.

What is needed to give further credibility to these kinds of performance-based assessment? For a beginning, each school or school district should develop some consensus on the criteria for evaluating students' work and some formulation of clear, consistent, reliable methods of reporting—to the students, the parents, and ultimately to the larger community.

These are challenging tasks; they will not be accomplished quickly; they will not be accomplished by teachers isolated in their classrooms; they will not fit into a teacher's overscheduled, overworked school day. But this work is essential to meaningful school reform and to the concepts of shared leadership and decentralized school decision-making.

Schools must provide adequate meeting time and space for teachers and administrators to begin coordinated assessment planning. If teachers are to participate effectively in the shaping of instructional programs, then they must also be involved in setting standards for the kinds of in-depth, performance-based assessment that will be an essential part of the instructional process.

WORK IN PROGRESS

There is a growing body of research on work of this nature being carried out in several school districts around the country, and at the state level as well.

Since 1980, the Connecticut Assessment of Educational Progress program has used performance tasks on statewide student samples in art and music, business and office education, English language arts, science, foreign languages, and industrial arts. Among the specific performance tests: in foreign languages, a student writes a letter and speaks to an interviewer; in science, a student uses scientific apparatus and designs and conducts an experiment; in English language arts, a student writes two essays, takes a dictated spelling and word usage exercise, revises errors in focus, organization, support, and mechanics, and takes notes from a taped lecture; in accounting, a student makes journal entries and completes a payroll record (Marzano et al 1988, p. 138-140).

Richard Stiggins of the Northwest Regional Educational Laboratory reports,

> [N]early three quarters of the states are conducting statewide writing assessments based on a teacher's subjective evaluation of student writing samples. Trained raters evaluate overall quality, organization, style, content, and other key factors by applying clearly articulated performance standards in the process of evaluation. (Stiggins, 1987, p. 33)

The following are several examples of performance-based projects in progress in local school districts:

- *The Senior Project* at South Medford High School, Medford, Oregon, a teacher-initiated innovation described more fully in *NEA Today*, February 1989. The project is a three-part culminating activity that all 300-plus members of the senior class must complete in order to graduate. Selecting topics from any discipline, seniors must (1) write an 8-10 page research paper, (2) create a related project, and (3) make a presentation to a panel of staff and community members about their project, their research on it, and their personal growth. For example, a student interested in woodworking might research and write about Shaker furniture design, build a chair using this design, and present the knowledge gained during this experience to a panel of staff and community members who have knowledge of carpentry and woodworking.

- *Arts Propel,* a collaborative project in arts education for students ages 11-17 conducted by Harvard Project Zero, under the direction of psychologist Howard Gardner, Educational Testing Service, and Pittsburgh, PA, Public Schools. The program, which closely interrelates assessment and curriculum, engages students in a series of exercises involving critical understandings and practices in a particular artistic domain. Assessment focuses not only on what a student produces, but on the processes of learning and production. An essential assessment device is the portfolio, which contains full process-tracking records of student involvement in one or more art works—for example, initial plans, drafts, self-evaluation, feedback by others, the completed work, and plans for subsequent projects.

- *The Exhibition of Mastery,* a fundamental theme of instruction and assessment in Ted Sizer's Coalition of Essential Schools. It includes a variety of methods—timed tests, essays, oral exams and presentations, debates, recitals, field projects, and portfolios of work—by which students, in a final exit-level "demonstration," may show that they possess the intellectual skills, the judgment and know-how to apply what they have learned, and that they are ready to graduate from high school and assume the responsibilities of working or college life.

- *The Key School Project,* Indianapolis, Indiana, planned by Patricia

Bolanos, the elementary school principal, and seven teachers, based on Howard Gardner's Theory of Multiple Intelligences. An inner-city "option school," Key integrates assessment and instruction in the arts, language, computing, as well as the "basics." Each child is expected to complete three projects related to a school-wide theme, which is selected for each of three nine-week periods. The completed projects are videotaped and placed in the individual child's portfolio. Patricia Bolanos (1989) says, "Everything we're doing is work in progress. We're working at changing our report card, getting away from standardized grades. Howard Gardner is helping us develop an assessment instrument to use with this work."

These diverse initiatives share a determination to link curriculum and assessment, to provide numerous ways of engaging students and a variety of ways for them to demonstrate understanding, and to obtain multidimensional accounts of student progress. If assessment intends to learn about what students and teachers have accomplished in school, these projects suggest some intriguing paths toward such a goal.

REFERENCES

Bolanos, P. 1989. Telephone interview with author, January 1989.

Madaus, G.F. 1988. The influence of testing on the curriculum. In *Critical issues in curriculum* (87th yearbook of the National Society for the Study of Education, Part I), ed. L.N. Tanner, 83-121. Chicago: University of Chicago Press.

Marzano, R.J.; Brandt, R.S.; Hughes, C.S.; Jones, B.F.; Presseisen, B.Z.; Rankin, S.C.; and Suhor, C. 1988. *Dimensions of thinking: A framework for curriculum and instruction.* Alexandria, VA: Association for Supervision and Curriculum Development.

Stiggins, R. J. 1987. Design and development of performance assessments, a National Council on Measurement in Education instructional module. *Educational Measurement: Issues and Practice* 6 (3): 33–42.

Stiggins, R. J., Rubel, E. and Quelmalz, E. 1988. *Measuring thinking skills in the classroom,* Rev. Ed. Washington, D.C.: National Education Association.

Wiggins, G. 1989a. Telephone interview with author, January 1989.

Wiggins, G. 1989b. Teaching to the (authentic) test. *Educational Leadership* 46 (7): 41-47.

3. MULTICULTURAL EDUCATION: A CURRICULAR BASIC FOR OUR MULTIETHNIC FUTURE

by Carlos E. Cortes

On January 18-19, 1990, representatives of California's public and private universities held a statewide conference to address the need for improving teaching preparation in the areas of ethnic diversity and multicultural education. While participants generally voiced support for the conference theme, Celebrating Diversity, a problematic undercurrent pervaded the gathering. As voiced in the session at which I spoke, that concern went as follows—"I believe in the idea of multicultural education, but what exactly is it?"

On February 10, 1990, scholars, writers, government officials, and other concerned citizens met at the statewide Envisioning California conference. Once again the issue of multicultural education arose, this time in my session, "Perspectives on a Multicultural Society." One of the more provocative challenges came from Jim Quay, Executive Director of the California Council for the Humanities, who asked—"What knowledge, skills, and attitudes do people need to live together successfully in a multicultural society?"

On February 23-24, 1990, teachers, administrators, and parents of the Minneapolis School District's Hans Christian Anderson School Complex worked together intensively for two days as part of their year-long endeavor to chart directions for creating a Multicultural Gender Fair Laboratory Demonstration School. As keynote speaker, I was charged with addressing the question—"What should be our vision for such a future-oriented school?"

In three different settings—a meeting of persons involved in teacher education, a conference of concerned citizens, and an elementary school planning retreat—participants had recognized the importance of orienting education toward our multiethnic future. Yet in all three settings, participants struggled to find common ground concerning multicultural education, with three basic questions dominating. Why do we need multicultural education? What is multicultural education? And what should multicultural education strive to accomplish? I would like to briefly address these three questions.

WHY MULTICULTURAL EDUCATION?

Why do we need multicultural education? At least three imperatives provide the impetus—demographics, geography, and the societal curriculum.

First, demographics. Population projections suggest dramatic future changes in the multiethnic dimensions of the United States. In the fall of 1989 the U.S. Census Bureau predicted that while the white American population will grow by 25 percent between 1990 and 2030, during that same period the African-American population will increase by 68 percent, the Asian-American, Pacific Island-American, and American Indian populations by 79 percent, and the Hispanic-American population by 187 percent! The Population Reference Bureau has forecast that by the year 2080 the United States may well be 24 percent Hispanic, 15 percent African-American, and 12 percent of Asian ancestry. Rudyard Kipling once wrote, "All the people like us are We, and everyone else is They." For all of us, regardless of race, ethnicity, or national origin, "They" will grow in numbers.

Second, geography. Increasing diversity will occur in a nation which is becoming more densely populated. A century ago, in 1890, the U.S. government declared the official end of the frontier because we had crossed that momentous demographic boundary, two people per square mile—"congestion" from an 1890 perspective. At that time, the United States had 90 million people. Today California alone has nearly one-third that many, while the U.S. population, now 250 million, will soon triple its "congested" 1890 level. In short, Americans of diverse backgrounds must learn to live and work closer and closer together.

Finally, the societal curriculum. I developed that term as a metaphor for the massive, ongoing, informal curriculum of family, peer groups, neighborhoods, churches, organizations, institutions, mass media, and other socializing forces that educate all of us throughout our lives. Operating parallel to, sometimes competing with, and inevitably influencing schools, the societal curriculum continuously educates all people from cradle to grave. Much of that societal education, whether consciously or unconsciously, whether intentionally or unintentionally, concerns race and ethnicity.

Some elements of the societal curriculum contribute to interethnic understanding—families who raise their children to reject bigotry, religious leaders who foster respect for diverse ways of believing, youth groups that make intercultural understanding a centerpiece of their training, and public antiprejudice programs like the Anti-Defamation League of B'nai B'rith's national "A World of Difference."

Unfortunately, other elements of the societal curriculum work against interethnic understanding—families that foster racism, nativism, and religious intolerance; organizations like the Ku Klux Klan and White Aryan Resistance that champion hatred; and those "decent" folks (including some school educators) who close their eyes and ears to the existence of discrimination and take no positive action to oppose it (as Edmund Burke said, "The only thing necessary for the triumph of evil is for good men to do nothing").

Some elements of the societal curriculum teach for better and for worse. My own special interest, the mass media, provides a case in point. As I demonstrate in my book-in-progress on the history of the treatment of ethnic groups in U.S. motion pictures, at times movies have challenged bigotry and discrimination, while at other times they have served as textbooks for the expression of interracial and interethnic prejudice.

Schools, in other words, do not monopolize education about race and ethnicity. Societal multicultural education, both constructive and destructive, exists. Schools can only choose whether to participate in the multicultural education process or to leave that education to the

61

rest of society. Former University of Chicago President Robert Maynard Hutchins once said, "The best education for the best is the best education for all." In light of these imperatives, it is clear that the best education for all requires elevating multicultural education into a school basic for every student, as all will participate in our nation's multiethnic future.

WHAT IS MULTICULTURAL EDUCATION?

These three imperatives impel the development of multicultural education. Yet multicultural commitment, dedication, and action in response to these forces need to be guided by clear thought and careful decisions. As Aesop cautioned us, "Beware lest you lose the substance by grasping at the shadow." So let us briefly clarify that substance as the basis for effective action.

Christine Sleeter and Carl Grant (1987) have addressed the question of the multiple uses of such terms as multicultural education, multiethnic education, multiracial education, and bicultural education. By examining 89 articles and 38 books that employed these words, they developed a taxonomy of uses of the term, multicultural education. Rather than summarize that article or parallel Sleeter and Grant by identifying different things that multicultural education *is,* I will approach the issue from the opposite direction. Heeding Aesop's warning, I will suggest what multicultural education *should be* by contrasting it with what multicultural education *is not,* drawing upon my two decades of observations while working in curriculum and staff development with schools across the country.

Multicultural education *is not* merely the holding of ethnic food days, the celebration of ethnic or foreign holidays, or the commemoration of special group weeks or months . . . although these may be valuable components of a larger multicultural thrust. K-12 multicultural education should operate continuously, not sporadically; it should span the curriculum from kindergarten through twelfth grade; it should cut across subject areas; and it should be implemented throughout the school year.

Multicultural education *is not* the study of individual ethnic groups in finite, isolated units or courses . . . although these single group studies may be a very useful *part* of a broader multicultural approach. Rather, multicultural education should also involve the constant integration of the study of ethnic groups within mainstream courses and units in such areas as history, literature, and the visual and performing arts. As this is not an either/or issue, schools may choose to provide single group studies along with necessary multicultural curricular integration. For example, the study of U.S. history should continuously incorporate the experience of Asian-Americans, U.S. Latinos, and European-origin ethnic groups, while the study of American literature should include African-American and American Indian expression. However, schools may also wish to offer specialized courses on ethnic history and literature, or even the histories and literatures of single ethnic groups for students who want that intensive study.

Multicultural education *is not* the exclusive study of ethnic groups by members of those groups or by schools with large multiethnic populations. All students, regardless of the composition of their school, community, or region, need multicultural education that engages the full spectrum of our country's racial and ethnic diversity, because all students live in the same multiethnic nation. However, schools or districts may wish to give special emphasis, although not exclusive attention, to ethnic groups in their communities or regions.

Multicultural education *is not* simply education about ethnic differences, nor is it posturing about how all people are basically alike. Multicultural education should simultaneously explore similarities *and* differences. Students need to grasp both pan-human qualities as a basis for building bridges among people of different backgrounds, while at the same time students need to learn about the real and meaningful group variations in culture, race, and ethnic experience, which cannot be finessed by platitudes about how we are all basically alike or proclamations of color-blindness.

Finally, multicultural education *is not* simply education to reduce prejudice, although well-conceived, well-implemented multicultural education should improve intergroup understanding, leading to long-range and sometimes even short-range prejudice reduction. Multicultural education should not be viewed or evaluated as a quick-fix panacea for bigotry or as an inoculation against interethnic tensions in school or in society. After all, teaching language arts does not guarantee perfect literacy, nor does the teaching of mathematics guarantee universal student success in algebra or calculus. School education contributes to learning, including the development of interethnic beliefs and attitudes, but it does not control such learning. Such phenomena as racial, ethnic, and religious bigotry and conflict have existed for centuries, and schools should not be expected to "solve" problems that have eternally plagued and confounded humankind. Educators need to recall the warning of British historian E. L. Woodward—"Everything good has to be done over again, forever."

By contemplating what multicultural education is not, we can identify one underlying element that indicates what it should be. Multicultural education needs to be a continuous, integrated, multiethnic, multidisciplinary process for educating all American students about diversity, a curricular basic oriented toward preparing young people to live with pride and understanding in our multiethnic present and increasingly multiethnic future.

WHAT SHOULD MULTICULTURAL EDUCATION ACCOMPLISH?

Which brings me to the final question: What can multicultural education contribute to students and ultimately to society? Twelve years ago I wrote an article, "New Perspectives on Multicultural Education," (Cortes 1978) for the Association of California School Administrators' magazine, *Thrust for Educational Leadership.* In that article I posited the concept of the Multicultural Person—"a young person with the multicultural competencies (knowledge, skills, and attitudes) for living with effectiveness, sensitivity, self-fulfillment, and understanding in a culturally pluralistic nation and increasingly interdependent world." Effective multicultural education should help students progress toward becoming Multicultural Persons.

Let's put it another way. Suppose we could imagine our young people, of all races, religions, and national origins, receiving their high school diplomas, and we could wave a magic wand, transforming each graduate into a Multicultural Person. What multicultural qualities would we like them to have? With those qualities in mind as educational goals, we can more effectively multiculturalize our school curriculum.

So for the moment, let us dream. Or let me dream for you, by suggesting seven of the qualities of that 21st-century Multicultural Person, toward which multicultural education should strive.

(1) *An understanding of groupness.* Students need to understand the significance of groups, ethnic and otherwise. They should comprehend that all people belong to many groups, and that group membership influences (but does not rigidly determine) the ways a person thinks, acts, and believes, as well as the ways that a person may be perceived by others (for example, because of their racial or gender physical characteristics).

They should learn that while all groups have unifying elements, all groups also reflect internal diversity, and that group cultures do not remain static, but constantly change over time. Finally, as Multicultural Persons, they should recognize that a continually evolving knowledge of groups can provide clues to understanding persons who belong to those groups, but at the same time should learn to resist allowing useful, flexible group generalizations to harden into inflexible distortions of group stereotyping.

(2) *An understanding of both objective and subjective culture.* This knowledge of groups should include both objective and subjective culture. The study of objective culture—external elements like food, clothing, music, art, and dance—should be part of multicultural education. But to avoid superficiality, multicultural education needs to address subjective culture—a group's values, norms, expectations, and beliefs. In short, students should understand that every group has historically honed world views, and schools should develop student

abilities to recognize how people of different backgrounds may express these world views in distinct ways.

Recently while giving an intercultural teacher workshop, I noticed a posted list of rules for student behavior. One rule read, "Students will show respect at all times." Yet when I asked the teachers how they would know when students were showing respect, many were stumped. They had not considered the wide variety of cultural expressions of respect, or recognized that one culture's way of showing respect may be quite different from another's—for example, conversational distance, eye contact, body language, or the nature of responding when someone else is speaking. Multicultural education cannot transform students into experts on all cultures of our nation or the world, but it should help them, as Multicultural Persons, to become more aware of the presence of subjective culture, more insightful into others' world views, and more adept at understanding differences in actions as expressions of those cultures.

(3) *An ability to see the perspectives of others.* Related to subjective cultural world view is the presence of multiple perspectives. In Jean Renoir's film classic, The Rules of the Game, one character propounds a basic human dilemma—"On this earth, there is one thing which is terrible, and that is that everyone has his own good reasons." Throughout history, individuals, groups, and nations have had their own good reasons, even though others may disagree with them or even find their actions and reasons odious. A Multicultural Person should be able to identify, grapple with, and understand multicultural perspectives. Multicultural education should not champion the blind, robotic, amoral "acceptance" of all points of view, but should encourage the recognition and comprehension of multiple perspectives, even if this understanding ultimately leads to vigorous disagreement. Above all, multicultural education should help students learn to judge on the basis of evidence, not reject on the basis of prejudice.

What perspectives—by government figures, Japanese-Americans, and other Americans—make the World War II internment of Japanese-Americans more comprehensible, if no less reprehensible?

What perspectives did American Indians express when, in 1988, they erected a monument to Indian heroes at the Little Big Horn National Monument, and how do those perspectives contrast with traditional Custerian interpretations of that event? How and why has the U.S. Constitution been multiculturally reinterpreted and amended over time? A Multicultural Person should learn to confront these kinds of questions.

(4) *An understanding of our E Pluribus Unum heritage, both for the nation as a whole and for individual groups.* Cultures and multiple perspectives evolve from experience. In U.S. history, every ethnic group has undergone critical formative experiences, while these multiethnic experiences together comprise a central element of our nation's past. Through multicultural education, students should learn the nature and significance of these experiences... both Pluribus experiences of individual groups and the Unum experience of Americans as a whole.

Among these experiences, students should study the Pluribus relationships of ethnic groups to their root cultures—the significance of migration and immigration, the nature of contact with homelands, and the maintenance and modification of ethnic cultures through participation in the American experience. With such understanding, the Multicultural Person should be able to consider, with greater insight and sensitivity, the dynamic interaction between Pluribus and Unum in the present and the issues that this interaction raises for the future.

(5) *An understanding of the potential contribution that Pluribus can make to our society.* Multicultural education should go beyond addressing students' "roots" as a source of pride-building and intergroup understanding. It should go beyond addressing the "problems" that different ethnic groups have faced and currently confront. It should also expose students to the potential of ethnic Pluribus, in consonance with necessary societal Unum, as a source of national strength.

Pluribus enriches our society. It continually contributes to and modifies mainstream American culture—providing new perspectives and insights, adding new forms of expression, and building new global linkages. Pluribus also positions the United States to be a more effective nation on a shrinking globe, as immigrants, in particular, contribute cross-cultural knowledge and multilingual skills. The Multicultural Person should recognize the positive power of Pluribus that can operate hand-in-hand with cohering Unum.

(6) *Capacity to use, and not be used by, the media.* Too often overlooked, media analysis should become an important element of multicultural education. Given the inevitable, continuous operation of the media curriculum on race, ethnicity, and foreign nations, schools should help all students learn to analyze the multicultural content of the media. As part of critical thinking, students need to become more "media literate."

In my multicultural and global education workshops, I am constantly asked to elaborate on and provide additional training on media literacy, particularly the media treatment of ethnicity and foreignness (See, for example, Cortes 1980). For everyone, school learning will come to an end, but media learning will continue, so learning to learn critically from the media should become an integral part of the curriculum. Multicultural Persons need to be able to deal actively, analytically, and intelligently with intentional and uninten-tional media multicultural teaching, through the news media or through the so-called entertainment media.

(7) *Deeper civic commitment.* Finally, schools should attempt to develop in students a greater dedication to building a better, more equitable multiethnic society. This challenge goes beyond knowledge, skills, attitudes, understanding, and sensitivity. It goes to the heart of social commitment. The Italian poet, Dante, once wrote, "The hottest place in hell is reserved for the man who in time of great moral crisis remains neutral."

Future-oriented education for a multiethnic society and shrinking world, education for immigrants and native-born Americans alike, should strive to build a commitment to the pursuit of equity, not a retreat into the abyss of neutrality. It should propound a sense of multiethnic and global identity that goes beyond, without supplanting, familial, group, and national loyalties. Multicultural Persons, in short, should have a concern for others as well as for themselves.

CONCLUSION

Diversity need not lead to divisiveness. But the failure to promote intercultural understanding virtually guarantees societal division. Multicultural education must not be viewed as a short-range program for solving societal problems, eliminating prejudice, or eradicating intergroup conflict. It cannot resolve all of the issues related to American racial, ethnic, and cultural diversity, not to mention such other types of diversity as gender, religion, social class, region, and physical and mental differences.

But comprehensive, continuous, well-conceived, effectively implemented multicultural education can help make this a better nation. The challenge is tremendous, but the cost of failure is even greater. As Pearl Buck wrote, "All things are possible until they are proved impossible—and even the impossible may only be so as of now."

REFERENCES

Cortes, C.E. 1978. New perspectives on multicultural education. *Thrust for Educational Leadership* 7(3): 20-22.

Cortes, C.E. 1980. The role of media in multicultural education. *Viewpoints in Teaching and Learning* 56(1): 38-49.

Sleeter, C.E. and Grant, C.A. 1987. An analysis of multicultural education in the United States. *Harvard Educational Review* 57(4): 421-444.

4. FINDING THEIR OWN VOICES: CHILDREN LEARNING TOGETHER

by Peter A. Barrett

Schools are settings in which participants come face to face with texts, with others, and, perhaps, with themselves. Encounters with texts—for example, books, films, music—are usually and often excessively the focus of the curriculum (except in the case of music). Encounters with others—students, teachers, staff, administrators—are similarly inevitable. However, prevailing demographic patterns, school and classroom organization, and teaching methods can work to restrict who the other is in a particular place and the frequency and forms of interaction with that other. Less apparent in schools are opportunities for encounters with the self in a curriculum that invites and provides time for reflection, for challenges that go beyond academic demands, and for personal growth.

Inquiring into particular visions of schooling along the lines of self, text, and other can be useful in understanding the nature of those visions. More than just a teaching strategy or a method of classroom organization, cooperative learning embodies a vision of the learner as actively involved with texts and others, striving to achieve an authentic, personal voice that reveals and helps to shape the self.

The responses to my first questions—What did your group do well? What specific behaviors helped you complete the activity?—emerged haltingly, accompanied by the unmistakable aroma of the self-consciously "correct" answer.

"We worked to bring different ideas together."

"We discussed each question thoroughly."

"Everyone had something to offer."

The discussion quickly gained life and freshness when I asked the next question: What specific behaviors tended to get in the way of your discussions, to keep you from completing the activity in a

71

thoughtful way?

"Some of us were serious, but some weren't even involved."

"We kept getting interrupted."

"Yeah, our group kept changing the subject."

"And some people were always telling jokes, trying to be funny."

"Just trying to get attention."

"In our group, everyone would talk at once, so I might as well have been talking to the wall."

"Whenever we couldn't agree, we started arguing."

"It's hard to work with so many different ideas."

My fourth graders' comments about their cooperative work on a literature assignment that September morning picked up themes that had emerged when we reflected as a group on their first efforts roughly two weeks earlier. They found the going difficult, hampered by lack of agreement and resulting conflicts, by rapid-fire shifts in the discussion, and by an inability to concentrate.

Not a pretty sight. Proof that cooperative learning won't work, that we shouldn't risk it.

Or proof that we and our students have no other choice.

The students talked clearly and forcefully—and with some resentment at times—about their experiences as I recorded their remarks on the chalkboard. They spoke of engagement and focus, of audience, of ideas, of conflict, of otherness.

My response at the time was that their comments offered plenty of suggestions for specific group skills to work on in coming weeks. My realization now is that they had identified so many significant issues that we tend to avoid when we rely on more predictable approaches that appear to preserve our control over students' attention and the knowledge they attend to. My students' cooperative work and their ongoing commentary on that work suggest to me three such issues: first, the inescapable interaction with students of differing abilities, backgrounds, temperaments, and purposes, what I term otherness; second, the context of conversation in which that interaction proceeds and the importance of voice and audience within that context; and third, the effect of cooperative work on student dependence on the teacher.

At the center must be the notion of voice, regarded here as one's characteristic way of thinking and then speaking those thoughts with authenticity and vigor. Cooperative work thrives on the student's growing ability to use his or her own voice and to hear the voices of others as they work toward an interdependence of voices. Unlike recent texts on the teaching of writing, which have drawn skillfully on considerations of voice, the cooperative learning literature seems strangely, inappropriately silent. Whereas we may detect what a cooperative classroom or activity looks like—what the steps are—the literature regrettably offers few contextually rich examples of what such a class might sound like and how the voices in that classroom change over time.

Three of my fourth graders discuss Elizabeth Coatsworth's poem, "Swift Things are Beautiful":
   Geoff: Look! Look, but look at these things! Look at these! What I've noticed is, look, the first lines are like the same in both paragraphs, except --
   Mark: These things are fast; these things are pretty slow.
   Geoff: But look at the very last two sentences of each thing:
   The strong-withered horse
   The runner's sure feet.
   In unison: *And the ox that moves on*
   In the quiet of power.
   Chet: Let's look—
   Geoff: They're both saying, they're both saying that they have lots of power. These are both the same . . . practically. It's just that the horse and the ox and here they demonstrate the runner's sure feet.

In reflecting on their work, many of the students commented on the difficulty of working with other students, a theme not surprising in the early going and certain to persist even as they gain experience with cooperative groups.

Their concerns included engaging others in a positive way in the group's activities, handling the conflicts that inevitably arise, and dealing with the many ways of seeing when several students are at work together. This relentless otherness, so different from settings that isolate one student from another or put one in competition with another, is a critical characteristic of cooperative work. Perhaps such work reminds us that education is essentially a meeting, a conversation, a confrontation between two human beings. Fundamental to the process are the voices, spoken freely and confidently in the present in response to one another.

Huebner writes,

> The stranger, the alien, the enemy—anyone who is different than I am—poses an unspoken question to me, in fact to both of us. The question is why am I as I am, and why is she as she is? Her life is a possibility for me as mine is for her. And in the meeting of the two of us is a new possibility for both of us. The difference and perhaps the tension between us is an opening into new possibilities for us. Differences are manifestations of otherness. They are openings in the fabric of everydayness. (Huebner 1984, p. 115)

Lists of some of the "outcomes" from cooperative learning—accuracy of perspective taking, differentiation of the views of others, liking for classmates, and expectations for future interaction (Johnson, Johnson, and Holubec 1986)—only dimly suggest the possibilities discussed by Huebner. Perhaps his language—*the stranger, the alien, the enemy*—is too strong for us as we picture our classrooms. And yet so many of our students remain strangers from each other, if not enemies with, and strangers from us as well.

That inevitable otherness emerges through student-student conversation, another critical feature of cooperative work. By redefining the roles of teacher and students, cooperative settings alter the relationships within a classroom. Perhaps most important, the teacher no longer controls the conversations. The students no longer talk only to the teacher as sole audience, or to each other only *through* the teacher as some sort of gatekeeper, vying for the teacher's time, attention, and approval. Indeed, students speak, they converse with each other, in itself a fundamental change in the context in which learning proceeds in a classroom.

Mark: But, um, all right, that's all right, good, but let's look at the slow things.
And the ox that moves on
In the quiet of power.
Now the ox is moving in the quiet of power. What the heck does that mean? I guess the only thing I can figure is that they mean the ox is strong, pulling the cart—
Geoff: Yes, it says in the quiet of—
Chet: He's not moaning or anything.
Geoff: In the quiet of power.
Mark: Right, I mean quiet.
Chet: It's not moaning or anything.
Geoff: It has to mean something. You can't just say—
Mark: It's plodding on.
Chet: You can't just say, "Why, I'm moving in the quiet of power." Ha, Ha.
Geoff: It's like saying the quiet of power means the quiet of power.
Chet: Right, but we can't say that.
Mark: We've gotta have the meaning, you know—
Geoff: Like what is the meaning?
Mark: Like the ox moves on carrying his load. It's quiet, it's getting to be nighttime, the ox is moving on, and he's using his power, I guess. I don't know. I feel like we're stuck. Let's go back.

In observing small groups, even ones not structured in the ways some cooperative learning proponents might suggest, Barnes notes the emergence of a new communication system, "one which the children progressively shaped in the course of their discussions" (Barnes 1977, p. 79).

Here the children have gained some control over their use of language and the course their discussions might take. Barnes writes, "The more a learner controls his own language strategies, and the more he is enabled to think aloud, the more he can take responsibility for formulating explanatory hypotheses and evaluating them" (p. 29). As a result, the student enters into new relationships not only with the teacher and with the others in the group, but also with new experiences and new knowledge. As the conversation proceeds, the teacher can enter it by stressing what Barnes calls the *reply* function, in which he takes the student's perspective seriously and encourages him to continue with his inquiry, over what Barnes calls the *assess* function, in which he distances himself from the student and relies heavily on external standards of behavior. (Barnes asserts the importance of both functions.) (p. 111)

Barnes' notions of openness and exploration in student inquiry and the language that guides it find full expression in his argument that the curriculum is not simply "what teachers plan in advance for their pupils to learn." Barnes writes that teachers and students must enact the curriculum.

By 'enact' I mean come together in a meaningful communication—talk, write, read books, collaborate, become angry with one another, learn what to say and do, and how to interpret what others say and do. A curriculum as soon as it becomes more than intentions is embodied in the communicative life of an institution, the talk and gestures by which pupils and teachers exchange meanings even when they quarrel or cannot agree. In this sense, curriculum is a form of communication. (Barnes 1977, p. 14)

It is common to find in recent texts about the teaching of writing to children an important discussion of voice, a characteristic texture of an individual's writing that distinguishes it from another's writing. In spite of their usefulness, such discussions are largely absent from the cooperative learning literature. In a representative text, *Write from the Start*, Graves writes,

Voice is the imprint of the person on the piece. It is the way in which a writer chooses words, the way in which a writer orders things toward meaning. As writers compose, they leave their fingerprints all over their work. (Graves and Stuart 1985, p. 37)

Noting the artistic or personal authenticity implied by a strong voice, Graves laments its absence in the work of student writers, largely as a result of the severe criticism that greets students who attempt to put a personal stamp on their own work. "So gradually, from first grade on," he writes,

we start to knock children's writing voices out of them. By the time
they're seniors in high school, they whimper, or talk in a monotone,
or say nothing—just generalities. Generalities are a nice insulation
against insult. (Graves and Stuart 1985, p. 39)

When we speak of voice in writing, we rely essentially on metaphor.
In cooperative learning, too, we strive for ways to enable a student to
find his voice, not a metaphoric voice in this case, but his actual voice,
rusty from semesters of disuse, muffled by years of inattention, or
strained by a constant effort to have the class speak with one scholarly
voice. Graves refers to "intellectual ventriloquism" when the child
begins to write with the teacher's voice. Surely we need not restrict the
use of that particular metaphor to the child's experience with the
writing process. Given the opportunity, though, the student's voice
bears his otherness, offers his perspective up for consideration in the
cooperative group.

Mark: Now, "The pause of the wave." You don't see much pause,
do you, but when you look at it from a different point of view, you do.
Chet: But when it's coming towards you, it looks like it's pausing,
when it curls.
Geoff: No, no pause. . .
Mark: It curls over, then it crashes.
Geoff: No, there's quiet. A quiet pause and then, crash!
Mark: Yeah!
Chet: Oh, yeah!
Mark: Like that! It curves downward to spray. The curve of the
wave that's curving over you and then—
Geoff: And then you're dead, because you're suffocating under
the water.
Chet: No, Geoff. Be quiet.
Mark: And then it curves downward and when it crashes down all
the spray comes up.
Geoff: And also it breaks all the . . . I've been in some big waves
and it really breaks out all the—
Mark: Right above you, and it's curving over you, and it pauses,

77

and then crash and spray.

Implicit here, too, is the notion of audience. Just as earlier forms of composition instruction posited the teacher as the sole audience for a student's writing, traditional classroom settings make the teacher the primary audience for student talk, when it is permitted.

Rather than learning to respond to a specific set of instructions or a melange of red pencil marks, the student as speaker must intuit the meaning of the teacher's raised eyebrows or the leading, sometimes impatient responses to his statements. Cooperative learning provides new—and changing—audiences for the student, drawing him into conversation with his peers in settings structured by the teacher.

Barnes' sense of the importance of student talk in the construction of knowledge—that it represents a "major means by which learners explore the relationship between what they already know, and new observations or interpretations they meet" (Barnes 1977, p. 81)—is significant in this discussion of audience. He sketches out the link between an intimate or distant audience and the type of speech that occurs in each. He characterizes the intimate audience engaged in improvised, exploratory talk as the source of authority for the small group. He contrasts that setting with the distant audience in a full-class situation in which the teacher is the sole source of authority and speech assumes a pre-planned, "final draft" quality, that last term representing yet another link between voice in writing and speaking.

A group of children working alone is likely to find exploratory talk available to them if they know one another well. Equal status and mutual trust encourage thinking aloud: one can risk inexplicitness, confusion and dead ends because one trusts in the tolerance of others. The others are seen as collaborators in a joint enterprise rather than as competitors for the teacher's approval. (Barnes 1977, p. 109)

Removing the teacher from the position of sole audience also reduces the student's dependence on the teacher for guidance and approval, in speaking as in writing. My fourth graders and I do most of our work in literature, for example, in full-group discussions and in small-group (threes and twos) cooperative settings. The full-group work closely parallels the cooperative work; indeed, I often rely on initiatives and categories suggested by the students in full-group discussions when I structure the cooperative work. Nonetheless, a spirited group discussion can give way to rather desultory work in the cooperative setting. Some of the early small-group discussions were disconcertingly quiet. Small-group members can turn away from their partners and towards me for help with the directions, for assistance in resolving disagreements, and for reassurance about the correctness of their answers. No doubt assistance and reassurance remain important teacher functions even in cooperative settings. But they should—and will, in time—become important group functions, as well.

Our students do not become independent learners merely by learning more from us, as if a certain amount of knowledge or a certain number of skills frees them to set their own purposes and act on them, regardless of the settings in which they acquired that knowledge and those skills. Their purposes, instead, will emerge in their conversation, as they find their voices. Certainly the notions of voice and audience lead us to the development of the learner's sense of independence and the group's sense of interdependence. Cooperative settings work to free the students collectively from the academic and social constraints that characterize so many classrooms by fundamentally changing the relationships among all participants. They reduce dependence on the teacher, encourage positive interdependence on the part of the students, and foster a sense of accomplishment.

Mark: "The closing of day." The ending of the day. The sun is going down, the stars are coming out.
Chet: Yup.
Mark: "The opening of the flowers." Just like "Unfolding Bud." A flower that's opening.
Geoff: It's like she has her point of view. She's looking at everything that's beautiful.
Chet: "The ember that crumbles."
Mark: "The ember that crumbles." The ember in the fire.

79

Geoff: She might not be looking at things from a different point of view. She might be saying that everything is beautiful. It's just—
Mark: A matter of how you look at it.
Geoff: Beautiful in different ways, in different ways it's beautiful.
Mark: A fire is beautiful.
Chet: Different people think different things are, different, they see them in different ways.
Mark: I still . . . What you mean . . . Everything is beautiful and everything and, um, lots of things are beautiful and you don't have to, we don't have to know what you're . . . you can just look at it and it just looks beautiful to you, like a bunch of flowers, it just looks beautiful to you. Wait a minute! And there are some things that you don't really think of as beautiful and then they have to change your point of view.

The emergence of real conversation about academic matters within the classroom provides an important feature of cooperative learning. Bruffee (1984), meanwhile, relies on the notion of conversation on a much grander scale, but one that nonetheless captures our assorted themes. His analysis of the role of collaborative learning in the college classroom draws on Oakeshott's belief that it is their ability to participate in unending conversation—in public and within themselves—that distinguishes humans from other animals. He quotes from Oakeshott's *Rationalism in Politics*:

Education, properly speaking, is an initiation into the skill and partnership of this conversation in which we learn to recognize the voices, to distinguish the proper occasions of utterance, and in which we acquire the intellectual and moral habits appropriate to conversation. And it is this conversation which, in the end, gives place and character to every human activity and utterance. (In Bruffee 1984, pp. 638-639)

Building on Oakeshott's argument that thought is internalized conversation, Bruffee states that we learn reflective thought from social conversation. Indeed, rather than "an essential attribute of the human mind," thought is "an artifact created by human interaction. We can think because we talk, and we think in ways we have learned to talk" (p. 640).

Already the significance of conversation, of voice—our own and others', over time—is clear. Surely Bruffee's grounding in the college classroom need not deter teachers of younger students. Our students do not have to know more, to be older, to be drawn into this essential conversation. Bruffee also takes us beyond the position that cooperative learning changes merely the relationships within a classroom. He argues that it can change the substance of the learning itself. The traditional view of the authority of knowledge faces a challenge here in the form of knowledge as a social artifact established and maintained through conversation within an interpretive community that provides the individual, according to Fish, with a source of thought and meaning—and ultimately, of self (in Bruffee 1984, p. 640-641). Knowledge becomes socially justified belief rather than a solitary, individualistic enterprise. "To learn is to work collaboratively to establish and maintain knowledge among a community of knowledgeable peers," he writes.

> We socially justify belief when we explain to others why one way of understanding how the world hangs together seems to us preferable to other ways of understanding it. We establish knowledge or justify belief collaboratively by challenging each other's biases and presuppositions; by negotiating collectively toward new paradigms of perception, thought, feeling, and expression; and by joining larger, more experienced communities of knowledgeable peers through assenting to those communities' interests, values, language, and paradigms of perception and thought. (Bruffee 1984, p. 646)

As members of the interpretive communities that students hope to join, teachers draw their authority from a new source, quite different from that posited by the traditional view of the authority of knowledge. In turn, teachers are responsible for structuring effective collaborative learning experiences for their students, settings in which they can converse, engaging in the discourse employed by a particular community of knowledgeable peers.

81

Allowing our students to engage in conversation, to find their own voices in the context of cooperative learning, also invites us to listen to them more carefully. By providing new audiences, we become a new audience, with much to hear and much to learn about these individuals.

REFERENCES

Barnes, D. 1977. *From communication to curriculum.* Harmondsworth, Middlesex, England: Penguin.

Bruffee, K.A. 1984. Collaborative learning and the "conversation of mankind." *College English* 46(7): 635-652.

Graves, D.H., and Stuart, V. 1985. *Write from the start.* New York: Dutton.

Huebner, D. 1984. The search for religious metaphors in the language of education. *Phenomenology + Pedagogy* 2 (2): 112-123.

Johnson, D.W., Johnson, R.T., and Holubec, E.J. 1986. *Circles of learning: cooperation in the classroom.* Rev. ed. Edina, Minnesota: Interaction Book Co.

5. SCHOOL CLIMATE: THE OTHER CURRICULUM

by Dorothy C. Massie

Teachers surveyed in 1988 by the Carnegie Foundation for the Advancement of Teaching expressed faint praise—or less—for the results of the national school reform movement that dominated the education scene throughout the 1980's.

The 13,500 teachers surveyed for Carnegie's *Report Card on School Reform: The Teachers Speak* (1988) did give some positive marks to school reforms. They reported student achievement gains in mathematics, reading, and writing. Their responses indicated that goals at their schools are more clearly defined today than they were five years ago; that principals are playing more of a leadership role; that textbooks, and other instructional materials, and the use of technology for teaching have improved.

Still, most of the teachers took a dim view of reform results: Seventy percent said the reforms deserved no more than a "C" rating; 20 percent gave them a failing grade. Over half of the teachers said morale within the profession had substantially declined in the last five years (Carnegie 1988).

Why are so many teachers disenchanted with reform gains? Carnegie Foundation President Ernest L. Boyer, who wrote the opening section of the report, suggested several reasons: The reform movement has been conducted, he wrote, for the most part without teacher involvement. "[M]any teachers have remained dispirited, confronted with working conditions that have left them more responsible, but less empowered" (Carnegie 1988, p. 11). Those working conditions, the survey reveals, have included more red tape and bureaucracy for teachers, more political interference in education, more state regulation of local schools, more achievement testing, larger class sizes, and less time to prepare for classes and consult with other teachers.

"What is urgently needed—in the next phase of school reform—," Boyer concluded, "is a deep commitment to make teachers partners in renewal, at all levels" (Carnegie 1988, p. 11).

This commitment came to productive life in various school-based reform coalitions in communities around the country. Had the Carnegie survey concentrated on teachers involved in this second wave of school reform of the 80's, a far brighter picture of current school reform efforts might have emerged.

Teachers have been the planners, rather than the objects of reform in school restructuring efforts. This is a basic difference, but not the only one, between the various state-legislated school reforms of recent years, and the locally initiated restructuring projects at school-based reform sites. Harold Howe II wrote about why "homegrown" is better:

> I doubt that educational excellence can truly be legislated. Instead, I believe that excellence has to be patiently *grown* in schools that are given the resources to nurture that process. . . These building blocks are teacher morale, student motivation, parental interest, and a humane school climate supportive of learning. (Howe 1987, p. 202)

Increasingly, education theorists are learning what practicing teachers could have told them—and have probably tried to tell them for some time—that "legislated learning" is simply never going to happen. Any school reform measure, no matter how well meant or brilliant in theory, is doomed if its aim is to impose uniformity upon teaching and learning, if it fails to take into account existing school structures, or if it does not contribute positively to that hard-to-define mix of tangibles and intangibles—school climate.

Research on "effective schools" tells us that classroom climate in schools contributes to learning and that it is built upon shared values developed through consensus. In successful schools, these values include a strong sense of purpose and commitment to academic growth, an orderly environment, a perception by students that the

84

rules are fair and applied equally to all, and expectations for success—a clearly communicated belief in the students' ability to learn.

Judith Arter, writing for the Northwest Regional Educational Laboratory, points further to researchers' recognition that the existence of a climate that students, teachers, and administrators find satisfying is a reasonable end in itself and that next to the family, the school is one of the most important socializing agencies. "Thus," she concludes, "it is important to analyze what messages we are sending students" (Arter 1989, p. 1).

Charles Silberman said it most eloquently two decades ago, when he wrote in *Crisis in the Classroom*:

> Children are taught a host of lessons about values, ethics, morality, character, and conduct every day of the week, less by the content of the curriculum than by the way the schools are organized, the way teachers and parents behave, the way they talk to children and to each other, the kinds of behavior they approve or reward, and the kinds they disapprove and punish. These lessons are far more powerful than the verbalizations that accompany them and that they frequently controvert. (Silberman 1970, p. 9)

NEA MASTERY IN LEARNING PROJECT AND SCHOOL CLIMATE

> An ethos of proud individualism and personal achievement pervades this place and makes it a good American school.
>
> . . . From Profile of a Mastery In Learning School, December 1986

Development of the Faculty Inventory and the School Profile, the two earliest steps in initiating site-based reform at each Mastery In Learning school, required both serious introspection and active participation—the kinds of intense involvement that were as important, ultimately, to the climate of the schools as the resulting documents.

As these tasks progressed, several important things were happening—not all of them noted in the written agenda. Teachers whose crowded schedules and classroom isolation had limited their opportunities for collegial exchange to the hurried, sometimes desultory business of faculty meetings, or to sporadic encounters in lunchrooms and faculty lounges, were able to sit down together, many for the first time, and examine in an organized and comprehensive way all those conditions that comprised the particular climate of their school. Typically closed classroom doors began to open as faculties shared their professional concerns and understandings.

As the faculties worked together to develop program priorities and to investigate research findings on the goals they wanted to achieve, they came to realize that conditions in their schools were not static, but susceptible to change, to improvements they themselves could devise. School reforms need not always be imposed on the schools from outside the system, but could grow from teachers' own ideas, based on their own research, and on their first-hand understanding of the real problems of the school, its resources, its community, its unique character.

This rigorous assessment of the current realities of school life, measured against their informed vision of the best that schools can be—even before restructuring efforts began—had an enlivening effect on the teachers' morale, which in turn affected the way they regarded their work, their school, and their students.

Into Every Climate a Little Rain Must Fall . . . And an Occasional Storm May Help Clear the Air

The first part of the Mastery In Learning Faculty Inventory was a "Diads/Triads" exercise in which teams of teachers were asked to respond, and later compare their responses, to three questions about their school. To the first of these questions—*What is so wonderful about this school that you would never want it to change?*—many teachers spoke of the "friendly atmosphere" as a condition they would not want to change. Parents, students, faculty members, and administrators, all "got along well together," they said. But close examination of responses to other, more specific questions showed that this "getting along well" was largely social and, in professional matters, superficial.

This "friendliness" was reflected in an atmosphere—not unique to these schools—of almost excessive politeness. Schools typically seem to breed a cult of politeness, which impedes communication among colleagues and—because it seeks to evade, rather than solve school problems—works to the disservice of students. The other side of ultra politeness, of course, is not meanness, quarrelsomeness, or crudity; rather, it has to do with an honest, straightforward collegial relationship—an attitude of openness and trust, which implies mutual respect and which happens to be contagious, spreading from staff to students, to parents, and with careful tending, to all members of the school community.

Envisioning the Ideal School Climate . . .
Working to Get There From Here

> You share a vision of students who are "self-directed." You envision such students actively participating in the class, engaged in activities with you and small groups of other students that require complex and critical thinking. . . You describe yourselves as facilitators. You have a variety of materials to work with, all kinds of texts, source materials, computers. You stress your concern for the "whole child" in the whole school environment.
>
> . . . From Profile of a Mastery In Learning School, December 1986

Questions 2 and 3 of the "Diads/Triads" activity—*What is so bad that we should change it tomorrow? What problems need resolution but have no easy solutions and will require time for study?*—directed the teachers' thinking to the future. Typically, they identified the need to improve the physical appearance of their schools as a first step in improving school climate. As they turned to the long-range problems, they began the real work of envisioning the kinds of school reform that would contribute to a purposeful, productive, and humane school climate. This work has never ceased. As their restructuring plans have developed, participants have come to have a more realistic perception of the way their schools were, and more informed visions of what they want for the future.

Listed here are some of those visions. Some have been realized; others are still aspirations toward which the teachers and administrators are moving as they work to shape the culture and climate of their schools.

- *The school is a place of intellectual inquiry.* Teachers are challenged by their work; they regard themselves as lifelong learners in a community of learners.

- *The school has a shared sense of mission* that has been developed collaboratively. Faculty members know why they're there, where they're going, and what they expect the students to learn.

- *The school is student-centered.* Teachers have the time and commitment to see students as individuals, to recognize and respond to their different ways of learning, the different dimensions of intelligence. They work to create critical linkages between learning opportunities and student aptitudes and needs.

- *Teachers have high achievement expectations* for their students. They regard students with respect and with the clear expectation that students show the same regard for staff members and each other.

- *The school provides a "problem-solving" environment.* Classroom teachers, as well as administrators, have an "open-door" policy. Schedules and attitudes encourage teachers to use each other as resources, to share professional concerns, to energize each other.

- *The school is a place of visual variety,* esthetically pleasing. Cleanliness may be next to Godliness, but it's not enough: Classrooms, halls, assembly rooms, other spaces are colorful, attractive; they contain displays that show something about the character of the school, its idiosyncrasies as well as its achievements, what's funny about it, what's to be proud of, what's going on there.

- *Students freely approach counselors,* teachers, or the principal, for help or advice. Staff members listen. They are flexible and responsive when students consult with them.

- *Students, as well as teachers, are involved* in developing and enforcing the code of behavior. The rules are logical, fair, and equitably administered.

- *The school is orderly, but not grim.* There is a reasonable and healthy balance between the need for order and the spontaneity that is essential for creativity, critical thinking, problem-solving, and honest emotion.

- *Students are publicly recognized* and rewarded for accomplishments.

- *Academic and artistic accomplishments,* as well as athletic skills, are celebrated in the extra-curricular life of the school.

- *Parents are in the school*—as members of planning teams, as aides, as active participants in the education of their children.

- *The school is an integral part of the community,* sharing resources, forming partnerships with parent and other civic groups, and involving community members as volunteers in various school activities.

The list could continue: Teachers' aspirations for their work and for their schools are boundless.

The work of school-based reform is challenging, sometimes exciting, sometimes deeply frustrating. It is a task fraught with doubts, but there is at least one thing certain: It is a job that is never done. As Judith Arter has commented, "[S]chool climate improvement is not something that is done to fix the school so that it stays fixed. School climate improvement is a long-range process of becoming ever better" (Arter 1989, p. 2).

REFERENCES

Arter, J. A. 1989. *Assessing school and classroom climate: A consumer's guide.* Portland, Oregon: Northwest Regional Educational Laboratory.

Carnegie Foundation for the Advancement of Teaching. 1988. *Report card on school reform: The teachers speak.* Princeton, N.J.: Carnegie Foundation.

Howe, H. 1987. Remarks on equity and excellence in education. *Harvard Educational Review* 57 (2): 199-202.

Silberman, C.E. 1970. *Crisis in the classroom: The remaking of American education.* New York: Random House.

Part Two:
CONTEXTS

6. RESTRUCTURING: HOW FORMIDABLE ARE THE BARRIERS?

by Lynne Miller

My concern is barriers to school restructuring. Some of you might respond that there are no barriers and continue about your work. To my mind, such a position is foolhardy and leads to unfulfilled dreams and unkept promises.

I'd like to suggest some ways to think about barriers to school restructuring and then present cases of two restructuring schools, highlighting the barriers they are destined to face and some ways to overcome them.

THINKING ABOUT BARRIERS

When encountering a barrier it might help to envision a wall, a huge wall. One has two alternatives: To proceed at full speed or to take a detour. Given the peril of proceeding, detours are preferable. The road to school change is, more often than not, non-linear and leads to unmapped territory. As Edward Albee (1961) cautioned in *Zoo Story*, sometimes you have to go a long distance out of the way to come back a short distance correctly. When it comes to restructuring schools, it often makes sense to explore the unfamiliar, depend on intuitions, and discover new ways to get to a desired destination. The following understandings may prove useful to those engaged in restructuring efforts.

1. *Barriers are real.* They cannot be wished away. Peter Pan notwithstanding, the real world has to be acknowledged. Barriers are durable, often more durable than we are. We have to recognize this so that when we decide to take one on, we know that we might lose and the barrier might win. Barriers are perennial; they are part of the landscape; they never go away. No matter what we are trying to do,

team-teach in first grade or restructure a school, the barriers are going to be there. They appear and reappear with predictable regularity. We should be aware of their persistence, because it is a part of this process. When confronted with a barrier, some people run smack into it and hope to come out with minor injuries. In fact, much of the history of reform is marked by escaping with minor injuries and minor victories. When one chooses, however, to take intelligent detours, there is the possibility of achieving organizational health and long-term success.

2. *Barriers represent enduring tensions.* There are some tensions that are endemic to schools and to changing schools. An understanding of what those tensions are leads to an understanding of how to deal with them in a specific context.

For instance, there is a tension between product and process. One may have an idea s/he wants to put in place, as well as a process for putting the idea in place. What takes preeminence? Does one start with the product, the great design, or with the process, working together toward the great design? The tension is always there. Just as classroom teachers face the tension between teaching a common curriculum to all children and dealing with each child individually, schools also face tensions about when to push forward, when to hang back, when to take risks, and when to practice caution. The process/product tension lies in classrooms and in schools.

A second tension revolves around leadership, a question of who is really in charge, not just formally but informally as well. Who really makes things happen, and how do we work to make things happen? Leadership may be hierarchical or it may be democratic and participatory. It may be exclusively in the administrative structure or it may involve teachers and be dispersed throughout the organization.

A third tension deals with the focus of change efforts. Are we changing conditions for learning, or are we changing conditions for teaching? In every small step towards school improvement, and every large leap towards restructuring, that tension is present. Is change going to benefit teachers or children or both?

Finally, there is the tension around control. For example, there is lay and local control vested in school boards and there is professional control located in groups like teachers' associations. These two sources of control are often in opposition to each other; yet they must work together to achieve common ends. If schools are going to change, they must acknowledge the control that exists external to them and learn to win it over to their side.

A LOOK AT TWO SCHOOLS

Two high schools in northern New England—real schools given fictitious names here—are recent recipients of state grants to support their restructuring efforts. I'd like to describe each school's restructuring plan and then discuss the barriers they may face down the road.

Southport High School is located in a coastal community, which is suburban in character and which prides itself on the excellence of its schools. The district is considered a lighthouse for the state and the superintendent, the dean of school administrators. The school has 562 students, 50 percent of whom attend college upon graduation. The principal of the school is a man in his early fifties, who had long struggled with the inequalities he saw in secondary education in general and in his own school in particular. The vision for the school's restructuring plan is clearly his own. He stated publicly that he wanted to retire from the principalship having made high school valuable for all students. The school's formal vision stated:

> We want to develop a structure that will allow, indeed oblige, each teacher to commit to the success of all students (Southport 1988)

and that this commitment had a clear focus—the elimination of exclusivity:

> Exclusivity is detrimental to student success and teacher effectiveness. Exclusivity is dominant in secondary schools and makes it difficult to commit to all students. (Southport 1988)

The principal promoted the idea of developing heterogeneous, multi-grade teams to replace the stratified course structure of the school. The restructuring proposal he wrote with a group of like-minded teachers made reference to the work of Ted Sizer, John Goodlad, Phil Schlechty, Jeannie Oakes, and Robert Slavin as providing the rationale for moving toward the new team structure. A gradual approach to implementation was proposed. The first year of the project was directed toward putting a pilot ninth-grade team in place with the intention of moving the school toward 9-through-12 teaming over the course of the next four years. The proposal had the public backing of the superintendent and was approved by the school board as a comprehensive plan for changing the high school.

The team was designed for 70 students and four teachers and was opened to one-half of the entering ninth graders on a voluntary basis. The team was responsible for teaching the core subjects of English, math, social studies, and science during the morning from 7:30 to 11:15 A.M. In the afternoon, students left the team for electives or seminars. The seminars were designed as exploratory courses, often interdisciplinary in nature. While the students were in their electives and seminars, the team teachers had two and a half hours allotted to student services/conferences and individual and common planning. The team structure was intended to change the routines of school for both students and teachers.

Key to making the team concept work was reorganizing the way electives were offered. The principal argued that the conventions of high school scheduling presented the major obstacle to restructuring and, so, devised a strategy for what he called, "breaking the back of the schedule" (Fieldnotes 1988). Prior to the first year of restructuring, the principal introduced the notion of tandem teaching of multi-level elective classes. The elective teachers accepted this notion because it offered the opportunity to increase their sagging enrollments. In effect all "singleton" courses were eliminated and students had access to a wide range of electives throughout the school day, making the teamed core courses possible.

The restructuring grant proposal identified key areas for change: time, student placement, access to knowledge, curriculum, student-teacher relations, parent involvement, teaching methods, monitoring student progress, and teacher worklife. The initial emphasis was on time and student placement. It was assumed that if time were flexible, there would be opportunity for teachers to make the curriculum more connected and to experiment with alternative pedagogical practices. There was also discussion about developing thematic units, such as one concentrating on the river, once teachers had time to plan together, to use the four team periods to take field trips and to develop interdisciplinary projects. It was further assumed that heterogeneous grouping would provide access to a curriculum of value for all students, that the curriculum itself would become enriched, that student-teacher relations would improve, and that teaching methods would expand.

Westport High School is located in an inland community, just outside of its state's largest city. Long an agricultural center, the town has seen a migration of professional couples from the city, adding a decidedly suburban flavor. The school has 728 students, 68 percent of whom attend college. The district has undergone a major transformation under the leadership of its superintendent during the last five years and is becoming recognized as an innovative center— especially in the area of elementary education. The principal of the high school when the grant was written was a man in his early forties whose leadership style was informal and who handed much of his decision-making power to a group of teachers who dominated the school's staff development committee and who later formed the majority of its restructuring planning team.

The vision for Westport's restructuring effort was generated by this group of teachers. The vision was based on two beliefs:

Overall environment of a school is a key factor in facilitating student learning; schools have control over this factor and the learning process is best facilitated when all people actively participate and have a sense of empowerment over their learning (Westport 1988)

and was grounded on the assumption that, if teachers became

empowered to make decisions in the school, they would then empower their students. The emphasis was clearly on restructuring school for teachers as a precondition for restructuring school for students.

> In our restructuring, it is the active empowered professional staff that must make the decisions as to what the desired outcomes for students and functions of the school should be. Within the restructured school, all students would be empowered and be active participants in the learning process. (Westport 1988)

The teacher who wrote the grant proposal cited the work of Linda Darling-Hammond, Judith Warren Little, Donald Schon, Ann Lieberman, and Gary Sykes as providing the rationale for focusing on teacher professionalism and developing provisions for reflection and decision making during the early stages of the restructuring process. At the center of the project was the restructuring team. The school board was made aware of the proposal but took no formal action to endorse it or its implications for changing the high school.

BARRIERS DOWN THE ROAD

Having reviewed the formal plans for restructuring of two schools and the context of their renewal efforts, I'd like to make a stab at predicting the barriers each will confront in the initial years of their efforts.

1. *Product versus Process.* Southport, with its clear emphasis on program design, will most probably face a process barrier. In fact, this barrier has already appeared. There are four teachers working in the new team setting, but they have not been trained to teach in that way. Consequently, they don't know how to move from frontal teaching to cooperative learning. They don't know how to move from an orientation that treats kids differentially to one that treats them as if they were all capable of achievement. Southport has a product and it doesn't know how to put it in place. In fact, they've already committed themselves to a grand design without having figured out

how people will actually implement it. They have a problem they have to solve: How to incorporate process issues without losing sight of their larger mission.

For Westport, a major barrier will involve content. Critics will begin to say, "All right, you've sat around, and you've looked at your navel for three years, and what have you come up with in the way of something that's going to be better for children? What kind of program do you have?" It may well be the case that teachers will tire of reflection, or that reflection becomes so seductive teachers will lose interest in doing anything else. Down the road, the staff will have to deal with the need to integrate some product into their process. Both schools will have to figure out how they are going to deal with process/product barriers. To succeed, they are going to have to make some detours and invent new ways of reaching their destination. Southport is going to have to invent some processes to help put their designs in place. Westport is going to have to invent a clear, substantive focus. If the schools don't deal with the process/product issue now and devise strategies for navigating around the barrier, they will face more serious problems down the road.

2. *Leadership.* Southport faces a problem of ownership. The formal restructuring plan reflects the principal's agenda, and the principal is in charge. The minute the school tries to implement the plan, there will be a group of teachers who say, "I don't want to do it. It's your design; I think it's crazy. What's wrong with frontal teaching, anyway? That's the way I learned to teach. And not only that, some kids can learn algebra and some kids can't. It's your design!"

At Westport, nobody is in charge. If there are problems, who is going to accept the responsibility? Two years down the road the teachers may rebel against the Southport principal because he has forced his design down everybody's throat. And two years down the road, the Westport teachers may rebel against the Westport principal because nobody knows where he stands.

Another leadership issue could emerge in Westport if a clique of teachers assumes leadership without legitimacy. What if the restructuring team becomes the center of leadership for the school district?

Some teachers might respond, "You're not really a teacher anymore, you're really an administrator!" Suddenly "we" become "they." One of the issues in restructuring and in teacher empowerment is that teachers do not know how to be leaders, because they have never had the practice nor do they know how to treat their colleagues as leaders.

To circumvent the leadership barrier, Southport must start inventing ways to bring teachers into the process and help them learn new practices of shared leadership. It is going to be as difficult for the principal at Southport to share leadership as it will be for those teachers who are used to a charismatic, no-nonsense, visionary principal to assume it.

Westport, on the other hand, must figure out who is in charge of the project. Is it the principal? The restructuring team? Someone has to take responsibility for what happens. It is obvious that both schools will have to develop some form of collaborative leardership. However, the longer they are stuck in old patterns of behavior, the more foreboding the leadership barrier will become.

3. *Focus.* Southport has oriented its plan toward students. In the near future, Southport teachers might well remark, "As a teacher engaged in the restructuring program, I am integrating courses. I am learning about the river. I am meeting with kids. I am consulting. I am working with teachers in a collegial kind of way. I also have a spouse and kids and a life I want to lead and this is all for kids, and there is not a lot in it for me right now." To meet this challenge, teachers must find ways to use time within the school day for themselves. They cannot accept that there is going to be one period for student services, one period for consultation, and one period for team planning. They must take hold of the time allotted, make it their own, and have it serve their particular professional needs.

Westport, at the opposite pole, has oriented its plan to teachers. It will be more difficult as time progresses to convince people that a focus on teachers leads to any tangible pay-off for students. The Westport teachers will have to decide on a way to bring students into the restructuring agenda. If they fail to involve students, the barrier that an unbalanced focus presents may become so impenetrable that it all but destroys the restructuring effort.

4. *Control.* Southport wisely began its restructuring plan with full school board approval. Its initial meetings with parents further ensured a solid base of support within the community. If Southport is to continue to have widespread support, it must make every attempt to keep its constituency informed. In addition, it must present a "united front" to the school board and to parents. If there is one chink in its armor, given the power of the external community, the Southport restructuring project could find itself in difficult circumstances.

Westport did not begin with the luxury of full board approval for the entirety of its efforts, mostly because it didn't have a full plan to present. So much of Westport's proposal depended on emerging changes, it was difficult to communicate clearly just what restructuring the high school would require.

POSTSCRIPT ON THE TWO SCHOOLS

One may wonder: What *really* happened to these two schools? It is not often we have the benefit of hindsight. Having watched and studied the two schools for two years after making my initial predictions, I can report on the development of each school's restructuring effort, the barriers faced so far, and ways of handling them.

Southport

Southport's initial expectations were quickly and dramatically modified when it became obvious that parents and a large portion of the faculty were uncomfortable with the centerpiece of restructuring—the elimination of tracking. An early compromise, considered necessary to get the team concept going, was made, and it was decided to level classes within the team. Four teachers were identified as team members and plans were made to implement the ninth-grade experiment in September 1988.

The first year for the ninth grade team was fraught with problems

101

and possibilities. The problems centered on legitimating the team within the school. The team was viewed as a protected and favored sub-unit, having privileged status, and serving as a model for what the school was to become. Non-team teachers did not find the idea of teaming appealing; the principal's vision of the school was not shared; changing to a team approach meant giving up more than it offered in return. For the team members, the new approach held much of promise. They worked hard on curriculum and teaching and found in the new seminar program an area for experimenting with heterogeneous classes and interdisciplinary work. But the problems proved greater than the promise. In May 1989, the superintendent intervened and announced the team as it was then constructed would not continue into the next year. Rather, he instituted a plan whereby eight teachers would be teamed to teach the entire entering freshman class; students would not be placed in teams as previously. This new ninth-grade program would have as its major goal providing a transition year for students leaving the middle school and entering high school. No mention was made of changing the structure of the rest of the high school. In effect, what began as an effort to restructure the school became an effort to restructure the students, to help them adjust from the protection and security of middle school to the new rigors and demands of the high school. At the end of the school year, Southport's principal announced his intention to resign that position and return to teaching English at the school.

Westport

The first year's activities were somewhat diffuse as the restructuring team spent a large portion of its time on process concerns and data collection. Its efforts were further complicated by the arrival of a new principal, whose style and values were in marked contrast to that of his predecessor. The new principal, Mr. Carlton, had been an assistant principal at a high school in the neighboring city which was, itself, involved in a major restructuring effort that was part of Ted Sizer's Coalition of Essential Schools. Mr. Carlton's previous experience, and his personal values and beliefs, were antithetical to Westport's restructuring process. He viewed himself as a student advocate, a directive leader, and as someone who placed instructional change at the center of any school reform enterprise. He did not involve himself immediately in the restructuring project, but rather focused his initial energies on acquainting himself with the school and dealing with management concerns. His distance from restructuring was not unnoticed by the faculty, who were divided into two distinct camps, those who had thrived under the previous principal and those who had not.

The fragile peace that existed between the restructuring team and the principal was challenged when, after a year's deliberation, the team concluded that the teachers needed more time to plan before any action would be taken and recommended that students come to school one and a half hours late one morning a week to provide time for discussion and planning. The principal argued against the proposal, and with the assistance of the superintendent, suggested that the teacher time had to be related to something that would directly benefit students. A compromise proposal was ultimately presented to the school board and accepted. In the 1989-90 school year, the first and second quarters would be devoted to teacher planning for a student development curriculum. During that time, students would be released from their first and second period classes once a week to provide planning time. During the third quarter of the year, students would again be released from their first and second period classes once a week—this time to attend the student development class. During the fourth quarter of the year, business as usual would resume.

The plan for planning time and the teaching of a common student development curriculum was implemented with mixed results. A committee was formed to develop the curriculum, and all teachers were expected to teach the curriculum as it was written. Some teachers were comfortable with this approach; others were not. Student opinions were also mixed. The restructuring team continued to lock horns with the principal, who once again distanced himself from the process. Finally, the team submitted another plan for student development and teacher release time, which was accepted by the board. The restructuring effort got the go-ahead to continue into its third year.

Barriers and Detours

It is obvious that both schools faced barriers they didn't anticipate along the road to school restructuring. Some barriers proved more impenetrable than others; some were circumvented by taking inventive detours.

At Southport, the most formidable barriers were those of leadership and power. The principal was not able to share ownership in the teaming concept; as a result, the two groups undermined the project: Teachers who distanced themselves from the initial team and parents who had doubts about its potential for helping their children. In the end, the power of the parent group overcame the power of the principal, who resigned that post, and the plan was re-designed. This new plan may well address the issues of process/product and focus. Only time will tell.

In Westport, three barriers presented themselves. The emerging emphasis on product, in the form of the student development program, helped balance the initial focus on process and teacher worklife; the team managed to incorporate a concrete concern for students into its work. The student development program helped redirect the restructuring plan and established it on firmer ground. The leadership barrier was not so successfully circumvented. It still looms as a threat to the effort. The principal and the restructuring team are still locked in conflict. The team won the first round, in getting its proposal for student development approved. But there are more rounds to be fought.

Lessons Learned

I begin this essay by stating that barriers to school restructuring, or to any school improvement, are real and represent enduring tensions, and that school people have to acknowledge these realities and invent ways to get around them. To the extent that Southport and Westport were able to create new routes toward these ends, they were able to keep their visions alive and their projects progressing. To the extent they were overly controlled by their original itineraries, they found themselves "stuck" and unable to reach their goals. How formidable are the barriers to restructuring? They are very formidable. How surmountable are they? They are surmountable, given the right combination of persistence, adaptation, and invention.

REFERENCE

Albee, E. (1961) *The American dream and the zoo story: Two plays.* New York: New American Library.

7. DINNER AT ABIGAIL'S

by Madeleine R. Grumet

Abigail's is perched opposite the shopping mall on Routes 5 and 20 just inside the town limits of Seneca Falls, New York. It is a large, white sided, rambling place, set off from the road by a large, gravel parking area that can easily accommodate the regular meetings of the town's Kiwanis and Rotary Clubs. Exempted from the precious self-consciousness of nouveau cuisine, Abigail's dinners are disarmingly generous. Relish trays, soups, salads and desserts appear, as a matter of course. So it was during dinner at Abigail's, ordering the onion soup, passing the relish and the rolls, that the faculty of Mynderse Academy figured out how to work together.

Mynderse Academy is a high school involved in a restructuring project. I, then a professor of education at Hobart and William Smith Colleges, was the consultant to the project, which encourages and supports teacher development, empowerment, and curriculum change, and requires that teachers get together to determine what they need to do to improve the learning environment, politics, and curriculum of their school. Implicit in the agenda is the assumption that what goes on in the classroom is linked to what goes on in the corridors, the lunchroom, the principal's office, the teacher's rooms, even the buses.

We held meetings in the library after school at first. Representatives to the steering committee came when they could. But it was difficult. They were tired, had to leave for other meetings, were reluctant to give up sessions set aside to help students with class assignments. Nevertheless, we persevered, trying to shape the project with whoever was there, but it didn't start to come together until we had dinner at Abigail's. Certainly, we can attribute some of the success of that dinner to the renewed energy we all felt given a few hours between teaching and reconvening. We can attribute it to the amenities of this welcoming place, to the raising of glasses, and ceremonious passing of the rolls and the relish. Over the years some of us had come often to Abigail's with our spouses, with our families to celebrate birthdays, graduations, anniversaries, even those Thanksgivings when we didn't want to cook. So I will grant that, along with soup and salad, Abigail served murmurs and memories of warmth and intimacy. Dinner at Abigail's may be merely one more instance of the contrast of recreation to work, of relaxation to tension, of intimacy to formality. But rather than accept these oppositions as necessary, I want to consider what it would take to move the energy, the confidence, and the fellowship that we discovered at Abigail's back into the cafeteria at Mynderse Academy. Sorry, Abigail. There will still be Kiwanis and Rotary.

In the early days of this century John Dewey taught us that the school should provide a model for the organization of a democratic society. He encouraged us to develop curricula that would provide children with structures for negotiation and decision making and with learning experiences that would help them develop the ethics and rational powers to participate responsibly in the shaping of their shared world. School, Dewey thought, is the place to practice making a better world.

Education is, after all, the process through which we take what is accidental and habitual in everyday experience and, with study and deliberation, choose what should be passed on to the young. Like Dewey, we continue to try to make our world better by educating our children to save themselves, and us, from the consequences of our mistakes. The child redeemer is a theme that runs through our culture as we prepare the next generation to deliver us from drugs, poverty, racism, and pollution. The education of these adorable saviors brings them from sentimental kindergartens and authoritarian classrooms to sun-dappled commencements where we exhort them to make the world a better place.

Our commitment to our children will continue to animate and direct our work as educators. Nevertheless, we have come to acknowledge that we cannot reform adult culture and society merely by manipulating the lives and relationships of children. If we accept Dewey's conviction that the school should be the model for a democratic society, then we must pay attention to the adults who open the doors, ring the bells, hand out the books and the homework assignments. And we need to pay attention not only to their relation to the children, but to their relation to each other, as well. What do they know of each other's work? When and how do they work together, if they work together? Do they know the parents of the children they teach? Do they want to know them and to engage them in this work of teaching their children?

THE ISOLATION OF TEACHERS FROM TEACHERS

In an era of increasing bureaucratization, when small businesses have been swallowed by large corporations, when office design provides cubicles without doors or windows, separated by flimsy room dividers, teaching "behind the classroom door" has extended an invitation that promises personal and distinctive practice. Many who rejected the depersonalization of business have been drawn to teaching, believing that it would offer them rich and vivid communication between teachers and students, as well as self-directed work. "Behind the classroom" door has become the phrase which stands for the privacy and intimacy that teachers may establish with their students when they close that door, construction paper taped to the glass, and get down to business.

Nevertheless, recent efforts to standardize curricula and teaching have seriously undermined this possibility of an individuated, self-determined way of working. The testing movement collapsed curricula into cram sessions. "Back to basics" brought with it a deluge of dittoes and of standardized materials. Centralized book ordering fostered a reliance on text books, which, when linked with standardized tests, obligated teachers to stick to the questions in their manuals. Even the talk between teachers and students, the conversation that might take place if the P.A. system was out of order, the

109

kids were not pulled out for "specials," and the door was closed, even that spontaneity has been squelched by those who took Madeleine Hunter's suggestions for curriculum and turned them into scripts for teacher talk and checklists of teacher evaluations.

As the individual intentionality and creativity of teaching have been appropriated by centralized administration, state testing agencies and book publishers, teachers have remained isolated, confined in their classrooms, without the compensation of determining the character of their work with the children they teach. This, as Sara Freedman and the Boston Women's Teachers Collective argue, is what burn-out is about. It is not about being overworked so much as it is feeling responsible for the experience of children and forbidden from shaping that experience. It is the frustration of being harassed and hampered by the organization of space and time and materials that are essential to your work without having any say about how the material resources that shape schooling are distributed.

In too many schools teaching is experienced as isolated and isolating work. Teachers just do not have very much to do with each other. The negotiations that they should have with each other take place instead with administrators, or just do not take place at all.

If teachers have been lured to the classroom by the promise, however false, of individualized, expressive work, they have been lulled into passivity, once they arrived there, by gender relationships that were shadows of male-dominated, patriarchal families. Too many elementary schools simulate these arrangements. Directed by male administrators, female teachers compete with each other for paternal approval. When their relationship does not degenerate into the petty squabbling of jealous sisters, teachers share their ideas almost surreptitiously. Given no time in the school year or the school day to talk to each other about their work, teachers find themselves hanging around each other's classrooms at the end of the day just to work out some of their concerns before they turn around and head home to the demands of their domestic lives and families. What they know about their work, what they have to teach other, their art and their science, remains sequestered in the confidences of friendship and rarely finds its way to the tables where policies are determined.

Although there is not space here to elaborate on the many ways that the culture of teaching encourages teachers to work defensively and alone, this brief mention of the themes that encourage isolation indicates that the intellectual and political loneliness of teaching is both encouraged by external pressures and exacerbated by teachers' reactions to those intrusions.

THE POLITICS OF TEACHING AND CURRICULUM

When teachers take back the prerogatives that have been abrogated by administrators, they are not merely satisfying their human needs for contact, for self-esteem and community, although these are all legitimate motives. The social and political isolation of teachers from each other also affects the knowledge that they are able to share with their students. Curriculum is not merely the syllabus. It is not only the reading list, schedule of tests, papers, and homework assignments. Curriculum is the way the world enters the school. It encodes the social relations, the power relations of people and knowledge. If those relations are seen as adversarial, split off and specialized, the world we bring to children becomes a jumble of walls and barriers and gates, and they must negotiate it as if it were an obstacle course.

Too many teachers assign papers or tests on the same night because they don't speak to each other. Too many teachers talk about events and things that are linked to each other in reality as if they existed in separate universes because they don't talk to each other. Too many elementary school teachers, who must teach several disciplines and could be sharing their expertise, offer shoddy instruction because they do not speak to each other. Pathways to a coherent world can be marked only by people who can speak to each other.

In high school isolation takes other forms. Often, male teachers, eager to disassociate themselves from the stigma that denigrates teaching as women's work, affect an exaggerated separatism. This desire to differentiate themselves from the culture of teaching and

111

from their women colleagues leads men teaching in disciplines that are traditionally male-oriented, such as math and science, computers, business and technology, and physical education, to also portray their disciplines as split off from the common discourse of the school.

In their attempts to ward off eroding waves of administrative intrusion, high school departments often become increasingly protective and self-interested. These characteristics, originating perhaps as defensive responses to social and political pressures, saturate the curricula of their disciplines, as well, fostering increasingly specialized and self-referential approaches to mathematics, literature, chemistry, or art.

Curriculum is not only an arrangement of knowledge. Curriculum is material. It takes place. It takes time. The arrangements of space and time that shape the class period, lockers slamming, papers out, bells ringing, get that assignment on the board, the details that determine the beginnings and endings, who sits next to whom, who gets to move and who gets a room with a view, all those details matter.

The faculty at Mynderse Academy understands this. They understand that critical thinking, writing across the curriculum, math and science literacy, all the new and desirable programs proposed for the secondary school curriculum must literally take place. They must work, if they are going to work at all, in Seneca Falls at 10:00 a.m. on a Thursday morning. And if they are then practiced in only one or two classrooms by courageous individuals, they will, in time, fail. For whatever goes on in one room must influence what goes on in all the others. As in an ecological system, a disaster or a miracle in any sector of the system will require notice and accommodations and in the others. So it is not enough to attend to the syllabus, the state requirements for graduation, test scores, and teaching methods. It is going to school and living and working in Seneca Falls that this faculty has begun to address.

At Abigail's, lured away from their offices, their classrooms and corridors, the Mynderse teachers leave behind the territories where their special interests are rooted. Around the long dinner table in Abigail's back room, people begin to talk about the issues that their departments face. Teachers from English, from music, from social studies and physical education listen to the representatives from the chemistry department talk about what it means to their curriculum to have their lab periods reduced. Teachers from the physical education and technology departments agree not to denigrate each other's agendas in their attempts to get rooms back from a plan that would collapse both programs into one room.

When issues such as these stay in the discrete departments, the faculty is divided into competing interests, just as Machiavelli counselled. Then the general good is distinguished from the particular good. The principal or the superintendent, administrators who are not entangled in the lives of individual students, stand up for the common good. The teachers, those with intimate knowledge of the students, negotiate only so far as the limits of their courses or disciplines permit. Their access to the "whole child" or the "whole curriculum" is ceded to the administration. When they challenge administrative decisions they are reminded that only the administrator's views and concerns are comprehensive. Only when representatives from all the faculty meet and discuss their needs and commitments can the faculty forge an opinion that can address the good of the school.

Dinner at Abigail's not only brings members of different departments together, it also brings them out of the school and into the world. For too long, contact with the "outside world" has been owned by the front office. Denied phones, opportunities to leave campus for an hour or an afternoon, denied sabbaticals and leaves, the very teachers whose work it is to introduce our children to a complex world are themselves exiled. Perhaps, if we were all more comfortable in the world we have made for ourselves, we would be less ambivalent about bringing our children into it. The schools we build to introduce them to the world more often function like a cocoon and keep them out of it. Sequestered and infantilized, teachers and students yearn for color, for context, for conflict, for purpose. Abigail's may not provide a Cajun festival, an Italian block party or even a "power breakfast," but it is out there in the same world where we all live. Curriculum is about the world and curriculum needs to be negotiated in and through the world.

The new superintendent of Seneca Falls knows this. After Abigail's we asked for time, time to meet during the school day. He arranges to send the students home early two days a month. We plan to meet in the cafeteria. It's not Abigail's, but it's the first time that the district has acknowledged that its teachers need and deserve time to work together.

The superintendent responds to the messages that the world sends him: "effective schools" literature, dire pronouncements of national reports on schooling, regulations, lists and standards promulgated by the state. Kids graduating from this school district, he tells the faculty, will either have to get a regents diploma and go to college or they will have to develop a skill that will get them a job. They will send the non-regents kids to the B.O.C.E.S. to take vocational education courses. Sitting in the high school cafeteria, inhaling the lingering aromas of pizza and brownies, the teachers try to keep the local students (that's what we call the non-regents kids) in town. If they go to B.O.C.E.S., they will spend two hours a day on the bus and necessarily become marginal and intermittent visitors to the community of their own school. It is almost 3:30.

Teachers are starting to leave, first the coaches, then others. Three years since the National Commission on Excellence in Education reports, and the war against Toyota is still being waged in the Regents Action Plan, in standards for high school graduation that ensure higher dropout rates, and in the splitting of the school population into vocational and collegiate tracks. Casualties of the campaign for excellence are nominated to spend two hours on the bus for courses in cosmetology and auto mechanics when only 35 percent of these vocational students will end up employed in the trades for which they have abandoned general education, the soccer team, the school play, and the promise of promise. Not all the teachers leave. Some stay. The talk that follows could be called political or it could be called pedagogical. How could we get statistics from the NEA on vocational education to counter the superintendent's ideas about B.O.C.E.S.? Should we contact the curriculum committee of the board, or make a statement at the public board meeting? None of the parents of the non-regents kids were on the board or came to its meetings. Who could identify them and alert them to what would happen to their kids if this went through? Could we convince the faculty to form a curriculum council so that the departments could pool information and interests and develop a school-wide concern for programs that would prevent a divide-and-conquer approach from the administration? Research, public relations, policy making—all the processes associated with administration were being claimed by teachers working desperately to educate their students.

Clyde Collins, who chairs the project steering committee, addresses the next working session of the faculty. "With these meetings," he tells them, "we are moving from a collection of autonomous individuals with little internal communication to a faculty that utilizes a collective approach to education at Seneca Falls." He challenges his colleagues to take up the project of making and re-making policy:

I'm not sure of the solution, but it would seem that some kind of faculty group needs to be created that would review curricular concerns with administration and the curriculum subcommittee of the School Board to instigate action, not just to respond to action taken or proposed. We need to view each change as a research project that needs to be evaluated to judge its success or failure and make proper revision. The whole educational setting should be constantly evolving as is the community. This should be a guided process by the faculty, administrators and School Board. Teachers need to be respected for our judgement and expertise as educators. Some of this need can be met when we are allowed to create the setting for education and then assume some of the responsibility for success or failure, growing professionally as programs are reworked. Teachers as a group, given the time and place to communicate with each other, know more than any administrator whether a program is working, and what needs modification. We hear the diverse comments of students, parents, and citizens. We as a group, have years—decades—of experience in the community and know its needs as well. I believe that a faculty that has ownership of its programs will work to improve them, but a faculty that never knows when its labors will be for naught will resign itself to mediocrity.

A curriculum council has been formed to provide a forum for issues of interest to the teaching community and to communicate faculty opinion to the board of education. The council has met with the curriculum committee of the school board and has made presentations at public school board meetings. The council has started its own research project to investigate the value of the in-house programs in business, home economics and industrial arts to its graduates. You can hear the conviction of collective concern in this statement written by Marge and Don Fahrenholz, teachers at Mynderse Academy:

> Seneca Falls was a college town with several large industries. The college closed, the hospital no longer functions, a large industry has relocated, and our school system has changed with the changing population. It now has fewer students of high-academic achievement but rather is noticing a shift to students with special educational needs.
>
> An attitude has existed in this community for many years which was based on past scholars. One student who graduated several years ago from Mynderse, has worked at the White House for the President and is now in the Treasury Department. He is cited as an example of the type of student Seneca Falls has. While many graduates of Mynderse have gone into prestigious positions, no mention is ever given to the students who dropped out of our school because it was no longer functioning for them. These students have not dropped out of town, they are still here working in one of the local factories. You can walk through Goulds Pumps and meet these people anytime. They vote on the budget and they remember.

If you have wondered why teachers, who already are burdened with large classes, time-consuming study and research, exhausting bureaucratic and disciplinary tasks, why these teachers should desire to assume some of the responsibilities that have been the province of administrators, the passion of this statement may provide your answer. No good teacher merely teaches a discipline, a body of knowledge or

116

subject matter content, even though we are often encouraged to think of teaching as merely the careful delivery of precious objects. And teacher empowerment does not require the development of group process or leadership skills. Teachers are informed, concerned and mature citizens. Provided with conditions that permit them to work together and to address the real issues that face them and their students, teachers can and do change schools. Teaching is about how to live in the world. And it is by working together to share and shape the world of their students that teachers act and teach responsibly.

BIBLIOGRAPHY

Carlson, Dennis. "Teachers as Political Actors: From Reproductive Theory to the Crisis of Schooling." *Harvard Educational Review,* Vol. 57 No. 3 August 1987, pp 283-307.

In laying the basis for a view of teachers as an important force for transformative change in the schools, Carlson also reviews the historical development of teachers' professional and trade-union movements, locating them in a general analysis of U.S. work culture.

Freedman, Sara. "Weeding Out Women from Women's True Profession: Burnt Out or Beached" in *Changing Teachers, Changing Lives.* Len Barton, Ed. London: Open University Press, 1987.

Freedman addresses the irony of criticizing teachers for the state of the curriculum when teachers have not been allowed to take responsibility for its form or content. She offers a critique of the treatment of teachers in the school reports and argues that burn-out is a form of blaming the victim.

Grumet, Madeleine. *Bitter Milk: Women and Teaching.* Amherst, Massachusetts: University of Massachusetts Press, 1988.

How is teaching meaningful to us as part of our private and public projects to create and support a new generation? The influences of gender and parenting are explored, both in their presence in the lives and work of individual teachers and in the ways that schooling in this nation has developed in response to these human commitments.

Kliebard, Herbert M. *The Struggle for the American Curriculum.* Boston: Routledge & Kegan Paul, 1986.

Kliebard traces these themes in the evolution of the American curriculum: the work and thought of John Dewey, vocational education, activity curriculum, scientific curriculum-making, social reconstructionism, and life adjustment education.

Lieberman, Ann, Ed. *Rethinking School Improvement.* New York: Teachers College Press, 1986.

In this collection of essays addressing school improvement, chapters by Maxine Greene, Huberman and Miles, Lieberman and Miller, Schwartz, and Jacully-Noto and Passow raise interesting questions and possibilities for teachers to direct the development of curriculum and schooling.

Maeroff, Gene, I. *The Empowerment of Teachers.* New York: Teachers College Press, 1988.

Maeroff reviews the conditions of and constraints on the work of teachers and details the new programs initiated across the country to acknowledge and support the leadership of teachers in curriculum reform and development.

Weiler, Kathleen. *Women Teaching for Change.* South Hadley, Massachusetts: Gergin and Garvey, 1988.

Weiler examines the experience of women who, as teachers and administrators, work to change the conditions of their work and the character of the curriculum. She addresses these teachers' efforts to develop a critical consciousness of the political and social forces that are shaping their lives and the lives of their students.

8. FOOTPRINTS IN THE SAND?: DOCUMENTING SITE-BASED SCHOOL REFORM

by Carol C. Livingston

An important tenet in the school restructuring movement is the concept of local determination and site-based decision making. School districts throughout the nation are experimenting with various forms of school-based management. Several major national networks have been created to support comprehensive school-based school reform. These include the Coalition for Essential Schools, the National Network for Educational Renewal, and the NEA Mastery In Learning Project and its successor, the MIL Consortium. Many of these projects deviate dramatically from the prevalent trend toward the industrialization and standardization of education (House 1986). It is essential that these projects and others like them be documented and evaluated for their efficacy to be established and for their experiences to guide others (Sirotnik 1987). The means to accomplish this evaluation, however, are problematic. This chapter describes the efforts of one of these reform projects to document its processes and outcomes. It elaborates, through concrete examples, the reciprocal nature of the documenting process and the development of norms critical to self-renewal at the school level.

DOCUMENTATION/EVALUATION FOR FACULTY-LED SCHOOL RESTRUCTURING

Educational decision makers express increased dissatisfaction with traditional evaluation designs because the largely quantitative evaluation information fails to help them *understand* how to improve programs (Datta 1982). This criticism is particularly acute for renewal and reform projects. Most traditional approaches to educational evaluation sample only minimally the data relevant to school improvement and fail to account for the complex interactive conditions encountered in changing educational environments. Most important, the very concept of standardized and externally administered program evaluation is antithetical to the process-oriented and site-specific nature of these reform projects.

Fundamental to the notion of school-based school improvement is the principle that every educational decision that can be made by a local school faculty, should be made by that faculty (e.g., Sarason 1971; Bentzen 1974; Goodlad 1984). Such decisions require informed inquiry and critical thinking, an evaluative process which is an ongoing part of the worklife of the professionals in that school. Participation in "evaluation," then, is integral to the process of school improvement (Sirotnik 1987). Evaluation must be interactive and reactive, not external (Kemmis 1986). It must be ecologically sensitive and acknowledge that goals are part of the system, not external to it (Stake, Shapeson, and Russell 1987).

Clark (1987) proposes that documentation generates such formative evaluation data and helps to provide "institutional memory" that can benefit both project participants and others who engage in similar endeavors. Multiple sources of data (e.g., documents, interviews, site visits, surveys, and student data bases) and multi-level documentation (e.g., by central project staff, project consultants, and school faculties) provide a rich information base for comprehensive analysis and feedback into the system.

Additionally, documentation needs to address the interests of various levels of stakeholders. The last decade has witnessed a shift in governance from local to state dominance. Public confidence in educational decision making has faltered. Frazier (1987) discusses the critical importance for educators to collaborate with state governments to establish a self-correcting process that monitors system quality and has high integrity with the public. He suggests we take qualitative "snapshots" of exemplary schools to "demonstrate to the legislatures, governors, and the general public that the education community deserves partnership status" in decision making (p. 112).

Mastery In Learning's Documentation Design

Mastery In Learning's documentation design attempted to incorporate an ecological model of evaluation into its documentation process. Intended to serve both central Project and site-level evaluation needs, the design called for four types of data collection: 1) benchmark data about the school, 2) a process record, 3) products, and 4) documentation interviews.

Benchmark data: School Profile and Faculty Inventory. Data from each of these initial activities (see McClure, Introduction) were used in initial planning and filed for future reference. Several MIL schools created interim measures based upon or adapted from these initial sources.

The process record. MIL participants were asked to keep a paper trail of Project activities: memos, minutes of steering committee and sub-committee meetings, and other records.

Project products and artifacts. Each school was encouraged to identify a historian who would keep artifacts, often including a scrapbook, of Project activities and accomplishments.

Documentation interviews. Faculties were asked to identify a documenter to conduct three cycles of interviews with a sample of the faculty each year. The purpose and procedures for these interviews and their analyses were adapted from the ethnographic tradition. A manual and videotape were prepared and disseminated to provide training and guidance for this activity. Site-based Project consultants were encouraged to participate and provide assistance.

The interview questions were designed to elicit perspectives about dimensions of school improvement identified as essential in the MIL philosophy: Attitudes/perceptions and outcomes/accomplishments about the production and use of knowledge and about the school itself (teaching, learning, climate, and program). The sample of faculty interviewed each cycle was to include a core of "regulars," and to involve both group and individual interviews. Interviewers were encouraged to fine-tune questions or probes to suit their specific

121

situations and to follow any developing themes or patterns. They were to work with a recorder to capture literal content and then record their reflections and interpretations. At the conclusion of each interview cycle, the documenter was to discuss the emerging themes with the steering committee to inform ongoing Project planning. Additionally, they were to report the results of each cycle in an interview with a staff member from the central Project office.

Other documentation sources. Supplementing the documentation described above were analyses by site-based consultants (most notably through end-of-year reports) and formal and informal analyses by central Project staff (including notes, conference and workshop presentations, articles, speeches, and requests for targeted information).

This documentation design would seem to provide a useful album of "snapshots" for documentation and assessment at local site and national Project levels. The central Project set up a generalized process with many options and avenues for specific documentation foci to be shaped by local sites. In practice, however, there was wide variation in the quality, form, utility, and utilization of data collected in and across schools.

The Extent and Nature of MIL Project School Documentation

Central Project. In reviewing the documentation evidence filed in the Project's central office at the beginning of the third full year of MIL, we became aware that the type, amount, and comprehensiveness of data varied greatly by school. In some instances the major summative data source, the end-of-year report, had not been submitted by the site consultant. Some folders contained a strong process record of minutes and correspondence, while others did not. All but four schools had reported at least one documentation cycle, but only two had reported four. As a gross indicator of quantity of data, the folders ranged in thickness from one-half inch to over six inches.

We were aware that some of the data we received did not find its way to the school folders. For example, the monthly newsletter column and the editor's source notes were rich data sources, as were research reports, conference papers, and articles for publication about MIL. Of course, the collective staff memory contained much that was never formally documented.

At both the local school and the central Project levels, the needs of the action present were always the most pressing. Particularly in situations where resources of time and energy were scarce, documentation was oft-forgotten. School leaders and central Project staff faced competing demands for their energies, and it was not always possible to provide the necessary monitoring, assistance, and encouragement. We were, however, aware that there were schools with documentation efforts that were not reflected in our "central" collection. We wondered about the status of on-site documentation.

Local school sites. We asked each steering committee chairperson to complete a survey detailing the types of documentation kept by the faculty. Categories included Faculty Inventory and School Profile, other instruments and data collected, resource and knowledge-base materials, meeting minutes, other process data, written reports, schedules and chronologies, newsletters and publications, presentation materials, documentation interview data, student records, student products, faculty data, informal notes and records, media records, artifacts, and fund raising materials. Each of these categories was further subdivided. The results of the survey were summarized and tabulated. Although it was not possible to ascertain the completeness or quality of the actual data in each category, the schools' surveys indicated that, in general, faculties were documenting their Project activities and accomplishments.

Perception and Utilization of Documentation by Faculties

Knowing what faculties keep as documentation was only one issue. A school renewal focus demanded that we inquire into its use. To investigate the manner in which MIL faculties perceived and used documentation, we conducted a series of open-ended telephone interviews with site-based documenters, steering committee chairpersons, and Project consultants at each of the 26 sites. These interviews probed for types of Project information kept, the forms of communication about Project activities and accomplishments, the "evidence" of Project accomplishments, roles in documentation, and utility of the on-site interview and data-gathering processes for ongoing decision making.

The interview notes were analyzed for themes and patterns. These are reported in three ways. Three case exemplars illustrate the range of perspectives in data collection, perception of utility, and critical/formative impact in the context of the school and its unique characteristics. Next, those factors that seemed to encourage documentation are described, followed by those that seemed to inhibit documentation.

School A is a large, multicultural elementary school. Its Mastery In Learning Project had been a showpiece for the school, community, and teachers' association. There were identifiable initiatives within the school, and the faculty collaborated with researchers in a major research institution to pilot a new instructional program. The Project generated considerable pride among the faculty.

Several years into the Project, School A's new central administration requested that they provide evidence of the Project's accomplishments and effectiveness—something immediate and then a plan for assessment for the upcoming year. The superintendent was particularly interested in student outcomes. Project leaders were concerned that they had nothing to show. Some feared the superintendent was threatening their Project.

They called the central Project office with a plea for assistance in meeting their requirement. They hoped that Project staff would compile data and, in particular, provide them with a single instrument to measure the effectiveness of one of their initiatives. Faculty leaders were disappointed when Project staff offered, instead, questions about the faculty's goals and activities and a desire to help the faculty devise a strategy for ongoing documentation and assessment.

Why was this faculty stymied by a rather typical administrative request for accountability? The answer, in part, appeared to be that they had not systematically documented their Project plans, activities, processes, and accomplishments. Individual Project leaders made presentations about the Project, and there had been some media coverage, but archives were scattered among committee chairs and former leaders. There was apparently no central and easily accessible audit trail of minutes, memos, notes, committee decisions, or evidence of student outcomes with which to begin.

School A was actively engaged in restructuring, and the faculty was working toward collaborative governance. A mid-winter faculty retreat resulted in the formulation and writing of a school improvement plan for the upcoming year. Yet, full-faculty involvement could be characterized as sporadic. Without an established internal communication and feedback loop informed by regular process records and documentation, ongoing Project participation was limited. Many faculty members did not know what was occurring in the Project except as reported at the retreats. Consequently, there was little "collective memory" among the faculty with which to reconstruct an evidenciary account. It was unclear who could (or should) take responsibility to respond to the superintendent's request. It posed a burden and created a crisis of accountability.

Ongoing documentation was not perceived as a significant Project component in School A. Although a teacher had been designated "documenter" (interviewer), as Project guidelines suggested, she had never fulfilled this role. There was no time. Whether for the purposes of history, internal communication, formative feedback, or external accountability, Project documentation was not perceived to be sufficiently important to make time.

School A illustrates the fact that, for many faculties, documentation is an alien concept. Teachers' time is spent on the day-to-day work with students in schools. What time is available for Project work is precious; rarely is documentation perceived as useful, and certainly not immediately useful.

It is unclear whether this faculty perceived the lack of documentation as part of their dilemma. It appears that documentation remained an external (though unenforced) requirement.

School B. The site documentation survey illustrated that some MIL schools collected large quantities of material. The degree to which those collections contained meaningful (or potentially meaningful) data could not be ascertained from the survey. Analysis of the telephone interviews about documentation, however, suggested that the utility of the collections varied considerably across sites (and for faculty members within a single site).

Many of the well-organized collections were, at least initially, the result of individual historians or documenters who liked to collect and organize (the "philatelic" personality, if you will). Predictably, the collections of the elementary faculties appeared more "display"-oriented than those of secondary schools. School B's case illustrates how another elementary school responded to a mandate for documentation.

Like School A, School B, a K-through-5 elementary school, was surprised by a request to demonstrate their accomplishments and effectiveness. They had submitted a grant proposal for monetary support, and the proposal review committee wanted detailed information about the school's Project work. The initial reaction to the request could be characterized as, "We don't have any products; we don't deal in products." After initial trepidation, they set out to collect and assemble Project artifacts and documents from throughout the school. When the day came for the committee's visit, they had compiled and organized a display that filled the library tables. Using the collection, they described their Project and its various committees, and their goals, accomplishments, progress, and products. They received their grant.

Through this experience they became aware of the value of documentation for building support across multiple stakeholders. Their site-based consultant commented, "They have realized the value of artifacts in demonstrating concrete evidence of their activity to persons outside of the Project and to the lay-person outside of education."

Their record was undoubtedly easier to assemble than School A's.

They had an active historian who had begun a collection of items. More process documents were available because of their Project's effective communication link through regular dissemination of minutes, calendars of meetings, and other material to their full faculty; and because of the faculty's awareness of Project activities, it was easier to consult faculty members about additional evidence.

The experience of assembling this presentation changed their perception of the value of the collected material, sharpened their sense of what might serve as artifacts, and inspired new ideas about how they could be used. In a sense, the artifacts and process records helped them to anchor the abstract concepts on which the Project was founded (e.g., empowerment, faculty decision making, challenging regularities, and informed inquiry). Their experience and their collection of artifacts encouraged them to make presentations about the Project throughout the state. Their presentations, in turn, influenced the type of data collected; for example, they created a slide documentary of one of their initiatives.

Gradually, Project participants in School B realized that documentation is not the solo responsibility of any one individual. The importance of maintaining Project artifacts and process records was established; however, they still conducted the interviews more out of a sense of obligation to the central Project than out of a perception of local utility. For School B, documentation probably served more of an accountability than a decision-making function. Perhaps the function of documentation evolves over time.

School C is a rural middle school. From the onset of the Project this faculty was exemplary in its use of documentation for communication, decision making, and problem solving, as well as history. Although there was often a distinct philosophical split between teachers who questioned the necessity or advisability of changing schools and those who favored faculty decision making toward school restructuring, their effective use of documentation and assessment seemed instrumental in maintaining their "facultiness" and developing professional collegiality. It encouraged the provision of opportunity and formats to disagree amiably.

School C used the interview process from the beginning and maintained well-kept records. (Their interview record is so complete, in fact, that the Project consultant noted changes in the language and manner in which the faculty discussed themselves, their students, and their educational mission over the course of the Project.)

They established an active data collection, feedback, and discussion loop among the faculty. They regularly created instruments to survey students and staff about important decisions and to measure outcomes (programmatic and affective) of Project initiatives. Agreement was not a given, but the effective use of documentation and assessment kept the Project responsive and in touch with everyone's concerns, while providing support for controversial decisions.

They developed efficient and effective ways to communicate to multiple stakeholders—proactively. Their regular updates, which were sent to the parental advisory group and the school board as well as to the faculty, ensured support for Project activities and gave them communication channels which are essential in effective site-based decision making.

There seem to be a number of key reasons that School C was so successful in documenting/assessing their Project and why, in turn, their documentation was so influential in building and maintaining a successful Project. The critical reason is that documentation was perceived as an important Project function. The faculty (or at least the Project leadership) had an "evaluation mentality"—they sought and utilized assessment and documentation in their ongoing decision making. Documentation was not merely assigned to one or two individuals, but was a central focus. Another key to School C's success was that several individuals played key roles in the documentation process.

The Project consultant for School C was a university faculty member and researcher. Most significantly, she was skilled in ethnographic research methods and in facilitation skills. She provided organization, recommendations, modeling, and assistance to establish the responsive system of documentation, assessment, and communication. Critical to the future of the school's site-based decision making, she built capacity within the faculty and gradually changed her role from directive to supportive.

The documenter for School C was a special person, as well. She worked closely with the Project consultant and developed skills and independence. She recognized the sensitivity of the data, particularly the interview data, she handled, and developed a well-deserved relationship of trust with her peers on the faculty. Her role within the school (as a resource provider rather than a classroom instructor) was also contributory to the success of the documentation effort, because she had the flexibility to adjust her schedule for interviews, to meet with the consultant to analyze and summarize, and to meet with the steering committee to report and discuss. She knew that what she was doing was important, and she was willing to give of her personal time to accomplish it.

Finally, the site administrator was supportive of shared decision making and of the need to provide and utilize documentation. Flexible arrangements allowed for documentation interviews or special meetings; teachers sometimes covered a second class for such activities as films in order to release the teacher to interview. The principal also taught classes to release teachers to participate in documentation activities.

FACILITATORS AND INHIBITORS OF SUCCESSFUL DOCUMENTATION

These three schools illustrate the range of differences with regard to the role and success of documentation efforts in schools in the Mastery In Learning Project. Looking across the 26 sites, several patterns were noted.

Facilitators

Faculty documentation appears to be most successful in schools where:

(a) *Someone facilitated the process.* In sites where someone (generally, the site-based consultant) actively facilitated the collection and analysis of data and the communication of documentation results, the faculty was more likely to utilize and develop documentation. It was particularly helpful for this facilitator to possess skills in qualitative evaluation and to balance support with encouragement for the faculty to develop capacity and initiative for self-documentation.

(b) *Faculty members valued participation in a national demonstration project and understood their contribution.* Where faculties understood the importance of helping others learn from their experiences, they viewed the requests for documentation more in terms of contributions to the professional knowledge base than as impositions.

(c) *Faculties received administrative support including time and resources.* In sites where teachers and administrators worked jointly, the administrators (who, as a group, have traditionally been more conscious of program evaluation) lent their support to documentation efforts. The documentation process requires time that is already filled with a multitude of non-instructional tasks. Where time was provided, documentation occurred more systematically and with greater purpose.

(d) *Individuals were interested in systematic documentation.* A faculty's documentation effort was greatly facilitated when members were able to identify one or several individuals with a particular understanding of the value of documentation and a willingness to coordinate (but not usurp) it.

(e) *A sense of "facultiness" existed.* Contribution to and interaction with documentation data is a two-way and interactive process. Documentation was utilized most effectively in faculties where there could be open discussion of issues on which disagreement existed. "Learning to agree to disagree" takes time but is a necessary element of faculty reflection.

(f) *A structure for faculty communication existed.* Processes for communication within and across the faculty were essential for the dissemination of information, collection of documents and data, and reception of feedback. Forums and times for discussion of data, both at committee and full-faculty levels enhanced its utility and, in turn, provided feedback to sharpen future data collection.

Inhibitors

The process of documentation was inhibited where:

(a) *Faculties failed to value or use documentation data for Project decision making.* School A's case illustrates this pattern. The interviews suggested that this is not an uncommon starting condition, and that understanding grows gradually with successful experience.

(b) *Evaluation was conceptualized in "input-output" terms.* Changing and evolving programs cannot be judged with fixed and predetermined criteria. One manifestation of this conceptualization among faculties was the failure to acknowledge subgoals not necessarily specifiable in advance; e.g., that it may be proper for a committee to change course to pursue an intermediate and prerequisite issue, or that it may be proper to change or modify goals.

(c) *Documenters and consultants lacked training and experience.* Documentation methods such as interviewing, minute-taking, analyzing, and summarizing require skills which cannot be presumed. Without training, faculties may, for example, expend excess efforts in unnecessary detail, fail to document essentials, or record or relay information in a manner that causes distrust or resentment.

(d) *Organizational barriers existed.* Examples of organizational barriers included lack of time for interviewing, analyzing, reporting, organizing, etc.; lack of clerical support or time on equipment for production of notices, newsletters, updates, etc.; and inflexible schedules.

(e) *Teachers lacked leadership skills.* Without teacher leadership, efforts became fragmented and projects lacked focus. This was both difficult to capture in documentation and difficult (or too risky) for teachers to confront. In many cases, limited role perceptions diminished the likelihood of teachers seeking, valuing, or taking on new roles including those associated with documentation.

(f) *Documentation was used in power struggles.* When documenters or other faculty members became possessive of data or used the data selectively to further their own causes, the Project effort was set back.

131

Faculty members then became increasingly reluctant to utilize or contribute to documentation. There were similar results when documentation (particularly interview or survey results) was used to solidify the positions of the "us's" and the "them's" rather than to encourage open discussion and joint problem solving.

(g) *Teachers were reluctant to engage in constructive criticism.* The social norms of teaching often prevent teachers from inquiring critically into practice and developing professional collegiality. One of the teachers interviewed remarked, "Our [faculty] closeness was our greatest strength and our greatest weakness." Another reported that their documenter had resigned because she just "could not be a party to negative reports." The teacher explained, "We're very close."

(h) *Administrators were reluctant to share decision making with the faculty.* Where MIL was just "the teacher project," teachers had less of a sense of efficacy about their Project's (or their school's) destiny and sometimes failed to perceive any utility in documentation.

(i) *MIL central Project compliance demands were low.* The central Project's reluctance to demand compliance occurred on practical and philosophical grounds. An unintended, but inevitable side-effect of this stance was that the central Project failed to stimulate documentation and develop a functional awareness of its role in the school's renewal effort, particularly in the critical early stages of the MIL. A dilemma for any support organization (be it a central project or a school district) is the proper balance of support and challenge to develop self-capacity and inclination within the site.

(j) *Dependence on an outsider for documentation limited self-capacity.* A number of school sites relied almost totally on their site consultants for documentation. In general, these faculties did not appear to develop a capacity to conduct and use documentation. One school with an extensive documentation record on-site and at the central Project office employed an outside documenter (through grant monies). The data, however, were not used extensively in communication and decision making. In contrast, School C seemed to have developed habits of inquiry and documentation that will carry beyond the formal life of the Project. Their systematic use of data in consensus-building, accountability, and decision making should help them maintain continuous renewal.

CONCLUSIONS

Following the two-year period reported in this chapter, MIL's focus on documentation increased. Documentation interview questions were revised to reflect the concerns of faculties several years into the Project, and faculties wrote additional site-specific questions to probe areas of concern for their restructuring efforts. At the national level, a staff member was identified to coordinate documentation efforts. As part of a documentation and assessment pilot, representatives from five schools worked with a nationally prominent evaluator to assess their documentation endeavors to design approaches that captured the essence of Mastery In Learning within the uniqueness of their schools. Time was set aside at several national conferences to consider the facets and relevance of documentation and to collect cross-site data through the use of process models, event analyses, and case vignettes.

It has become evident that effective documentation of school restructuring looks different at each school. It should come as no surprise that a project that posits "every decision that can be made by a local faculty should be" would also encourage local decision making in the documentation effort. Although a national demonstration project must be documented, there remain dilemmas inherent in employing a single documentation design across sites. Common data are rarely "common." As an example, despite a common protocol, the form and content of the interview data varied so considerably that it was difficult to compare information across sites. Surveys told us little without probing the local conditions, experiences, and meanings behind responses. We discovered that documentation activities in conference settings provided valuable cross-project data.

One way other projects have answered the need for evaluation is to hire outside evaluators, documenters, or ethnographers. For this Project, however, (and for most small scale initiatives within and across districts), that was budgetarily unfeasible. Furthermore, for

MIL, the Project's commitment to site-based faculty design and implementation made external evaluators philosophically unacceptable.

In retrospect, what we might have done was more clearly delineate and emphasize the role of the Project consultant in helping faculties establish a documentation mechanism. Although the teachers hired their own consultant, a clearer notion of the consultant role may have facilitated the collection/production of documentation and enhanced its use in on-site decision making and the development of collegiality.

One recommendation we make without reservation is that there be training and at least periodic on-site support for effective documentation/assessment. Piscolish, LeMahieu, Johnston, and Young (1988) demonstrated that one means of complementing on-site documentation is through formal collaborative arrangements with local universities or research centers and labs. Such collaborative arrangements can be cost effective and provide evaluation expertise to the faculty. Care must be taken, though, that the agendas of each party are compatible.

Documenting school reform is not easy. But in MIL, Project "successes" clearly indicated that, where documentation was conducted and communicated on a regular basis, the process facilitated faculty building and "norms of collegiality and experimentation" (Little 1982). It enhanced the leadership and decision-making capacity of the faculties and encouraged the critical reflection necessary for self-renewal (Kemmis 1986; Sirotnik 1987).

REFERENCES

Bentzen, M. M. 1974. *Changing schools: The magic feather principle.* New York: McGraw-Hill.

Clark, T. A. 1988. Documentation as evaluation: Capturing context, process, obstacles, and success. *Evaluation Practice* 9(1):21-31.

Datta, L. 1982. Strange bedfellows: The politics of qualitative methods. *American Behavioral Scientist* 26:133-144.

Frazier, C. M. 1987. The 1980s: States assume educational leadership. In

The ecology of school renewal (86th yearbook of the National Society for the Study of Education), ed. J. I. Goodlad, 99-117. Chicago: University of Chicago Press.

Goodlad, J. I. 1984. *A place called school: prospects for the future.* New York: McGraw-Hill.

House, E. R. 1986. Evaluation and legitimacy. In *New directions in educational evaluation,* ed. E. R. House, 5-9. Philadelphia: Falmer Press.

Kemmis, S. 1986. Programme evaluation in curriculum development and innovation. In *New directions in educational evaluation,* ed. E. R. House, 117-140. Philadelphia: Falmer Press.

Little, J. W. 1982. Norms of collegiality and experimentation: Workplace conditions of school success. *American Educational Research Journal* 19:325-340.

National Commission on Excellence in Education. 1983. *A nation at risk.* Washington, DC: Government Printing Office.

Piscolish, M., LeMahieu, P., Johnston, J., and Young, J. 1988. A collaborative model of program evaluation, administration, and policy development: The Schlenley High School Teacher Center experience. Paper presented at the annual meeting of the American Education Research Association, New Orleans, LA.

Sarason, S. B. 1971. *The culture of school and the problem of change.* Boston: Allyn and Bacon.

Sirotnik, K. A. 1987. Evaluation in the ecology of schooling: The process of school renewal. In *The ecology of school renewal* (86th yearbook of the National Society for the Study of Education), ed. J. I. Goodlad, 41-62. Chicago: University of Chicago Press.

Stake R. E., Shapeson, S., and Russell, L. 1987. Evaluation of staff development programs. In *Staff development for school improvement: A focus on the teacher,* ed. M. F. Wideen & I. Andrew, 196-212. New York: Falmer Press.

9. PERSONAL AND PROFESSIONAL RENEWAL THROUGH ELECTRONIC NETWORKING

by Shari Castle, Carol C. Livingston, and Beverly Johnson

> New knowledge . . . emboldens teachers to think, to examine their practice, to believe that they are competent to change existing practice. And there is an almost electric sense of energy that accompanies this realization, a sense of excitement that raises the energy level throughout each building. (Thompson 1989, p. 91)

RESEARCH-PRACTICE INTERACTION

Problems persist in using research in school settings and in sharing the largely uncodified wisdom of practice. Using the knowledge base is a task for which teachers often have too little time, access, and understanding (Berliner, undated) and too few models that link research to contextual factors affecting the change process. Empowering teachers to use a constantly growing knowledge base requires (among other things) contextually sensitive research utilization models (Shulman 1987). Teachers use their experience to mediate between generalized research findings and application in specific situations (Schnesk and Rackliffe 1989). Yet neither the practical wisdom of teaching experience nor this application process has been codified. Electronic networking, such as the IBM/NEA School Renewal Network, is one attempt to explore the use of theory and research, good ideas, and practical wisdom by researchers and practitioners across a broad geographic area.

THE IBM/NEA SCHOOL RENEWAL NETWORK

The primary purpose of the School Renewal Network is to create an interactive research base on school restructuring among a community of actively engaged practitioners and researchers. The Network is designed to address the following needs:

a) location of and access to research and other resources,
b) interaction between researchers and practitioners around the use and generation of research on school reform innovations,
c) dialogue about issues central to school reform work (such as site-based decision making),
d) data gathering and analysis, and
e) efficient communication across Mastery In Learning schools.

The School Renewal Network, an asynchronous teleconferencing and messaging system using PCs which began in October 1988, represents the first electronic network dedicated specifically to school reform. Network participants include the 26 Mastery In Learning schools, seven federally-funded research laboratories and centers, seven major universities, and seven schools from other networks (The Coalition of Essential Schools, The National Network of Educational Renewal, and the NEA Learning Laboratories).

IBM provided hardware, software called PSInet (People Sharing Information network), and technical support. NEA's Mastery In Learning provided personnel, overhead, demonstrations, initial training, information resources, and server maintenance. Each site provided a Network coordinator, training for faculty members, and telephone costs.

Grant funding from the Secretary's Fund for Innovation in Education at the Office of Educational Research and Improvement enabled further development of the Network. Participants focused the research-practice dialogue by selecting and defining 10 critical topics and engaging a researcher for each topic. The critical topics represent some of the major school reform issues: parent involvement, at-risk students, curriculum design, positive school climate, school/classroom organization, instructional strategies, thinking, networking, restructuring, and authentic student assessment.

Gary Watts (1989) captured the importance of the Network as he spoke metaphorically of two great rivers converging:

> River number one . . . is the nation's . . . conception of what a teacher is. The teacher is becoming a professional decision-maker. River number two [is technology]. What's the power of the second river? The ability to retrieve, sort, compare, prepare, store, display, and share information has been dramatically increased because of the power of the computer. The confluence arrives at a point when [the professionalization of teachers] needs support and encouragement and help and technology to . . . expand the capabilities of the individual. The utilization of the technology to enrich human capital . . . We need to find how to move research horizontally to teachers rather than vertically down through the tiers where it gets peeled off as it goes down. The IBM/NEA School Renewal Network is our means. It is a unique and extremely significant experiment.

Examples of Interaction

Significant increases in use, depth of content, researcher participation, and researcher-practitioner interaction have occurred on the Network (Castle, Livingston, Trafton, and Obermeyer 1990). The result is a database that is more comprehensive and more relevant to practitioner needs. Between January 1989 and January 1990, messages increased 20 percent, papers increased 161 percent, researcher involvement increased 26 percent, and reflective papers increased 11 percent. By January 1990, responses outnumbered requests for the first time, indicating a significant increase in contributions to the database.

Of the literally hundreds of exchanges that have occurred, one on student skill mastery gives the reader a sense of the Network at work on professional issues (All Network quotes are IBM/NEA School Renewal Network 1990).

3/3/90 CHECK Elementary School "Planning Reinforcement of Skills."
Steve Delozier

Here is something that I've been wondering.

Sometimes a student seems to master a skill today only to later forget how to do the skills in a month or two. On semester tests and year-end finals they don't seem to have retained as much as you thought. A year later teachers in higher grades ask, "How come these students can't do this skill? They should have mastered it a year before!"

To counter this, I give review quizzes every once in a while to reinforce earlier taught skills—mainly English, Math, Reading (mostly decoding and vocabulary—I know I need to review more on comprehension. I teach 3rd grade by the way.)

How long should this reinforcement go on for each skill? All year? Should I plan once a week for these review quizzes? Or would once a month be sufficient? How about daily boardwork where I include a few problems to review past skills? Should I concentrate on crucial skills? Am I just wasting time better spent on other skills???

I know it depends upon each class or individual (and I try to differentiate for this), but I'd like to know generally.

Is there any research on this?

I just want to know that I'm doing all I can do to prepare my students for skills to come in later years.

Do you keep reinforcing the skill throughout the year, or do you just reinforce until they are tested and then hope they retain enough to get by later? Maybe they don't master the skills now but will somehow pick up bits and pieces of the skill the rest of the year—enough to get by later. How do most teachers handle this situation? Any discussion? Is this a sticky question? What do you think?

[Steve Delozier, Check Elementary School, Check, Virginia]

3/25/90 GRIFFIN " 'mastery'? maybe not . . ." Skill Mastery, Testing, Retention

Some time ago, Steve Delozier at Check wondered electronically what's going on when students seem to "master" a skill only to later forget how to do it. The obvious solution, of course, is that the skill wasn't mastered at all—mastery defined as having the skill at one's command when it's needed, whenever that occurs.

Steve's dilemma is a common one for all of us and I think it points out dramatically how we are foreshortening the teaching-learning process. That is, we aim our instruction, hit a target, check for some sort of impact and move along to another issue. SLOW DOWN. PAY ATTENTION TO LEARNING AS CUMULATIVE AND ONGO-ING. USE MULTIPLE WAYS OF TEACHING AND ASSESSING. and so on.

Although I have some problems with the so-called process-product research on teaching, one of the important findings of that work was the central place that a sequence of "presentation, practice, seatwork, homework, assessment" plays in skill development (mainly reading and arithmetic). The main issue is that as teachers we don't give enough time to PUBLIC practice, practice that isn't worksheets or problems in a book or some other private activity—the latter is seatwork and is meant to give the student ample opportunity to repeat the CORRECT way of doing the skill until it's "mastered." Practice, on the other hand is done with the teacher's watchful eye and diagnostic mind fully engaged with the students' work—slip or a misstep or a puzzled look is a signal to the teacher during practice that instruction is needed, now.

What this research tells us is that it isn't enough to present material and have the kids do it on their own—we have to be there to be sure the students don't reinforce errors again and again. And we do that during (public) practice.

I'll bet that a bit more attention to this aspect of teaching would reduce the instances of Steve's dilemma.

Cheers, Gary Griffin [University of Arizona, Tucson]

3/28/90 CREMS "Skills Mastery" Skill Mastery Public Practice

I'd like to latch on to Gary Griffin's insightful comments on the need for public practice to give students ample opportunity to repeat the correct way of doing their skill until it's mastered.

Public practice under the watchful and helpful minds of teammates

141

is one of the major components of cooperative learning. Gary may have just put his finger on the most salient reason that cooperative learning improves student achievement and retention of knowledge.

John @ CREMS [John Hollifield, CREMS,
Johns Hopkins University, Baltimore, Maryland]

3/30/90 CHECK "R) Public Practice for Mastery"
to Gary G. and John H.
from Steve D.
re public practice

I plan out a time in the mornings and some afternoons when time permits for skill-related activities that I semi-supervise. (meaning that I listen to or watch the kids in these activities and notice which child dominates; which child has mastered the skill and now helps others to understand it; and which child answers incorrectly most often).

I step in to help some students individually, but I usually don't step in unless a whole group of kids does not understand the skill involved. Usually there are one or two students who have mastered the skill and help others to "practice" it correctly. If I hear a student "teaching" a student incorrectly, I will step in and review the skill with the group.

All of the materials that I let the students use are skill-related and will further reinforce skills to be mastered. I have flash cards, math bingo games, a variety of crayon/wipe-off games, and computer software—mostly MECC programs that are very well put together—all kinds of levels of skills. I keep a set near the computer for the kids to use during their individual computer time. I select the programs that reinforce skills we are currently practicing, as well as skills of which others need further reinforcement. I review the programs with the kids individually, so that they will know which level to start out on and then progress. I have also set aside a group of programs for the above average students (gifted)—these are some of my resources for differentiated plans for these students.

We also have started to get into some group activities during class time. We will play Jeopardy type games. The kids in the group have to talk over the answer to come up with a correct question. The groups are pretty heterogeneous, so the "masters" help the "pre-masters." They seem to handle it very well. I want to start getting into some higher level problem solving once they get used to working in groups.

Are these some correct measures to go about planning for "public" practice?

Steve Delozier, Check Elementary School

Beyond the Professional

Another example shows the personal and professional synergism produced by the network.

3/18/90 DFLEMING "Early Spring in Massachusetts"

In another conference, our colleagues are discussing "connected ways of knowing." In this paper, there is a hint of connected ways of living. It is offered up, in part, in celebration of spring at the forty-fifth parallel. Those of you who live in areas that are more southern or more mountainous or more west of the rockies are invited to share your lists, too.

MARCH-APRIL IN THE OUT OF DOORS (NEW ENGLAND VERSION)

Persons who are close to the earth read a clock that has no mainspring or battery. They are sensitive to the change in the winds, the roll of the clouds, the greening of the clumps of earth beneath the melting snows. They can feel the tick of time by reading nature. Change is not measured in minutes but in the shifting arrival of a flock of redwings, the opening of willow blossoms, the things in the out-of-doors. If you can read spring, you can read any time of the year at all.

1. Porcupines leave the hemlock and pine forests for a change of diet, moving closer to the edges of green meadows and roadsides.

2. Skunks leave circular dig marks in matted grass and pine needles as they search for grubs.
3. Male redwings and iridescent boat-tail grackles flock to the marshes and stake out their nesting areas.
4. Song sparrows begin to sing.
5. Woodchucks emerge from their burrows.
6. Summer robins, returned from the south, are shinier, plumper, and brighter than the robins who wintered here.
7. Raccoons prowl the back roads and forage in garbage cans or bird feeders.
8. Swarms of black midges hover in the air on warm days and evenings.
9. Spring peepers (Hyla crucifer) emerge and begin an incessant chorus.
10. "Bee flies" appear on the blossoms of willows. They resemble honey bees but cannot sting.
11. Poplars shake out their "tassels."
12. Snakes emerge from hibernation beneath ant hills.
13. Pickerel spawn in the grassy shallows of ponds and lakes.
14. The flowers of the Red Maple (swamp maple) appear long before the branches leaf out.
15. Violets bloom in meadows.
16. Marsh marigolds dot swamps and stream banks with bright yellow flowers and waxy green leaves.
17. Kildeer, Ducks, Geese, and Woodcock stop over on their journey north.

I used to develop lists like this for each month of the year. I'd use them with my students—as a way of inviting them to join me in the earth-watch too. Some of my students kept journals for a whole year. Others became field guides for classes in lower grades. A few assisted as trail guides at monthly walks conducted by our local conservation commision.

Here are some of the references I used to develop the lists and for enrichment reading or reading aloud.

Headstrom, Richard. THE LIVING YEAR. Ives Washburn, Publishers. New York: 1950.
Borland, Hal. SUNDIAL OF THE SEASONS. Alfred A. Knopf. New York: 1953.
Teal, Edwin Way. A WALK THROUGH THE YEAR. Dodd, Mead & Company. New York: 1978.
Candy, Robert. NATURE NOTEBOOK. Houghton Mifflin Company. Boston, MA: 1953.

[Doug Fleming
Regional Lab for the Northeast and Islands
Andover, Massachusetts]

3/23/90 PERRY "Thanks for NE Spring"

Hi Doug,
What a delightful list of "spring." It makes me realize that I haven't taken enough time to "smell the roses" in the Northwest. (One can call camelias "just around the corner.")

I'm going to share your list with the many teachers at Kimball who are interested in "Earth Day" activities and the environment around us. I'm sure Peter Hubbard could add a few colorful "spring" sights from his earthwork farm in the second grade.

Thank You!
Jan (KIMBALL)

[Jan Perry, Kimball Elementary School, Seattle, Washington]

3/24/90 AHUIMANU "response to early spring"

I enjoyed reading about your article on spring. It was so neat to read about all the different things that you can observe in Massachusetts . . . skunks, snakes, poplars, pickerel, raccoons. So many things that our children have never seen in Hawaii. What can we say about spring here in Hawaii? It all looks so much the same or so we think.

We need to take a closer look and be more observant.

1. Sixth graders start going wild . . . boys becoming girl crazy and girls becoming boy crazy.
2. Gardenias begin to bloom.
3. The golden plover returns to Alaska.
4. The humpback whale begins migrating back to the north Pacific area.
5. Flowers begin to bloom more . . . puakenikeni, plumeria, etc.
6. People are sneezing as avocado trees, mango trees, etc. are flowering.
7. The waves on the north shore are not as huge and the southern shore area becomes more popular for surfing and body surfing.
8. Fish prices come down as the more popular fish such as ahi are easier to catch.
9. Tourists begin to leave as the mainland starts to warm up.
10. Only light showers to bless the day so the children can go out to play.
11. The sun is up by 6:00 a.m.

I think this is a neat idea to do with the kids. I'm sure they'll come up with a lot more. Thanks, Max

[Maxine Haun, Ahuimanu Elementary School, Kaneohe, Hawaii]

3/30/90 CHECK "Spring signs in the Blue Ridge Mountains of VA"
Spring signs as seen by third graders in Floyd County, Virginia.

1. The grass turns green and grows and needs to be cut.
2. Various flowers bloom: Daffodils, Ladyslippers, Crocuses, and Apple Blossoms.
3. The robins and bluejays return from their vacation down south.
4. The crickets begin to chirp.
5. The grey squirrels start chattering in the woods.
6. The ground hogs emerge to look for clover.

7. The horses shed their winter hair.
8. The ants start invading the house.
9. The moles start digging tunnels in the yard looking for grubs.
10. The spring peepers peep at night keeping everybody up.
11. The deer start nosing around the fields.
12. The snow only lasts one day.

These are the things the kids noticed this year. They like being able to tell time without a calendar.

Steve Delozier, Check Elementary

3/25/90 GRIFFIN

The transcontinental and transoceanic correspondence about Earth Day and the exchanges of pleasure at the arrival of spring illustrate for me how important it is for educators and their students to open up to the world around them, their immediate surroundings as well as imagined or not-ever-thought-of-or-known-about "there" places. The hoopla surrounding earth day is important, not just because it helps us to focus, for a while at least (for a long while at best) on who we are in relation to our planet Earth. We do get imaginative on special occasions, don't we? What about the daily lives we lead with our students? Can we find ways to thread major beliefs, values, understandings, appreciations throughout our schools' lives together? What would our curricula look like if we chose to pay attention to the state of the Earth all year? For several years? Across all subject areas? In relations with our communities? In our sensitivities to one another? In our instructional materials?

The Ahuimanu example is a good one. The follow-up Reynolds extends to the kids' understandings (and, I guess, will raise some hard questions). Gary O.'s questions probably sparked other ways of thinking about Earth Day in Hawaii—they did in Arizona.

Speaking of Arizona, here are a few desert dweller's observations of spring in the southwest:

—the birds are back and hungry;

—the citrus trees are blossoming and their fragrance is everywhere;

—students at the university make elementary kids look calm at this time of year;

—contrary to common stereotypes, huge pots of petunias in all colors are brimming over and make great food for ground squirrels;

—temperatures are in the high 80's during the day and mid 50's at night;

—the coyotes are restless—every night;

—the desert plants do, indeed, bloom—including the cacti;

—and, as is true everywhere else, the work put off for a better day is no easier to tackle when the sun is shining.

Cheers, Gary Griffin [University of Arizona, Tucson]

Personal Renewal

A third example illustrates the personal renewal experienced through the network.

The Boca [Raton, Florida, Network Coordinators] conference really got me reconnected to my life's work in education. My energy and enthusiasm for all aspects of the job are far beyond what they were. I really believe that school renewal is a result, at least in part, of personal renewal. And the new information and questions that continue to flow into Kimball over the network are already making a positive difference. I'm really pleased to be a part of it!

[Bill Towner, Kimball Elementary School, Seattle, Washington]

CONCLUSIONS

We have drawn a number of conclusions from our investigation of the IBM/NEA School Renewal Network to date which might be of value to others engaging in similar networking ventures:

- *Planning and design.* A good start with proper support is essential because of the inherent dilemmas in a venture of this type. People will use the Network only if it appears useful; but the Network can't have any substance until people interact with and contribute to it.
- *Network structure.* Because the original sessions were not exhaustive of the scope of the four commonplaces, most papers were entered under a generic "information" heading, and the database became disorganized. The careful construction of the revised Network structure and careful definition of Network topics eliminated most difficulties.
- *Network coordinators.* Situations in which a single workstation must serve and involve many others require exceptional coordinators. They must be able to receive and to give training, convey the value of the enterprise to their colleagues, encourage involvement by others, and organize and disseminate information.
- *Time and access.* Time was, above all else, the major problem with the Network. Scarcity of time inhibits computer use, information dissemination, and faculty involvement activities. Inconvenient locations also inhibit use. In particular, limited access by other faculty/staff members necessitates the printing out of nearly all papers and the minimal use of the database functions of the computer. Network effectiveness (as judged by faculty involvement with the knowledge base) is thus constrained by the size of the faculty and the extent of their access to the Network.
- *Incentives.* Busy people need incentives to take on an additional, ill-defined, and complex task. Clearer definitions of roles, provision of stipends for Network activity, and camaraderie and shared purpose conveyed through the Network Coordinators Conference were incentives. These seemed particularly important in increasing the researcher role.
- *Connectedness.* A common purpose and links to activities outside the Network (e.g., conferences and newsletters) have strengthened Network impact.

149

- *Support and training.* Periodic training and face-to-face interaction are essential throughout the process. Content and process facilitators keep the dialogue moving and nudge or assist participants. Early support, in particular, must include prompt technical assistance on an as-needed basis for operation and hardware to prevent early discouragement.
- *Research-practice interaction.* True research-practice interaction requires the learning of new roles and skills, content relevant to both researchers and practitioners, contributions from both role groups, and a willingness to take risks. By nature, the specifity and focus of the contributions differ for the two groups. As the Network matures, it will be important to observe how these natural differences are accommodated in dialogue. As such, observation of Network activity may prove significant in understanding the elements of effective research-practice dialogue.
- *Network development.* Networks take time to develop, and they appear to progress through successive stages. In our first year, more attention was devoted to technical issues and less to substance. This pattern reversed itself in the second year. True dialogue takes time and support.

But there is something new here, something not at all prominent in early research on the diffusion and adoption of innovations: the belief that teachers have minds. It is as though, in the Wizard of Oz, the Scarecrow knew all along that he had a mind, while the Wizard came late to this conclusion. Well, the Wizards of Research know now that teachers have minds, and that teachers are pretty confident of that as well. (Thompson, 1989, p. 93)

REFERENCES

1. Berliner, D. (undated). *Readings in educational research: A series for educators.* Unpublished manuscript.

2. Castle, S., Livingston, C., Trafton, R., and Obermeyer, G. (1990). Linking research and practice for site-based school renewal. Paper

presented at the annual meeting of the American Educational Research Association, Boston.

3. Castle, S., Rackliffe, G., and Ward, N. (1988, April). *Teacher empowerment through knowledge: Linking research and practice for school reform*. Symposium presented at the Annual Meeting of the American Educational Research Association, New Orleans. (ERIC Document Reproduction Service No. ED 296 999)

4. IBM/NEA School Renewal Network. (1990). [Unpublished Network content]. Washington, DC: National Education Association.

5. Livingston, C. and Castle, S. (1989). *Teachers and research in action*. Washington, DC: National Education Association.

6. Schnesk, J. and Rackliffe, G. (1989). Faculty decision making: Sources of information. In C. Livingston and S. Castle (Eds.), *Teachers and research in action* (pp. 69-83). Washington, DC: National Education Association.

7. Shulman, L. S. (1987). Knowledge and teaching: foundations of the new reform. Harvard Educational Review, 57, 1–22.

8. Thompson, C.L. (1989). Knowledge, power, professionalism, and human agency. In C. Livingston and S. Castle (Eds.). *Teachers and research in action* (pp. 90-96). Washington, DC: National Education Association.

9. Watts, G. D. (1989). The confluence of two great ideas. Keynote addresses at IBM/NEA School Renewal Network Coordinators Conference, Boca Raton, Fl.

Part Three:
ROLES

10. THE DYNAMICS OF CHANGE: THE ROLE OF CHANGE FACILITATOR IN BUILDING COMMUNITY

by Marylyn Wentworth

School reforms in the past have been primarily the province of groups outside the school such as state or federal agencies and educational scholars and theorists, or those within schools in a position to mandate educational change. With the advent of school-based renewal, the impetus for change has shifted to the local school community. The involvement of all members of that community has become an important part of the processes and purposes of change. There is argument as to whether change occurs best when it begins with areas that directly affect student learning, or when the adults "get their act together" first by forming a strong, supportive, knowledgeable adult community. My experience tells me that strong adult communities support deeper changes for students.

Adult communities are not easy to build given the traditional patterns of schools. With the constraints of time and expectations, many contend that substantive improvement is best accomplished through the involvement only of those who are "true believers" in the proposed innovations. If part of the definition of community is inclusion, it is unlikely that any significant, long-lasting change will occur—in the structure of schools or in the basic beliefs about teaching and learning—without the involvement of the entire school community. Less than that fosters sabotage, resentment, or disinterest by those ignored, which cannot help but undermine any attempts at change in the long run.

The word *community* itself implies inclusion. This does not mean that everyone will, or even should be, in total agreement concerning

155

the nature of a school's work towards renewal. Positive dissent is an asset; it provides a valuable check-and-balance to the potential excesses, or simple wrong turns, of those who are eager for change.

Working successfully for school renewal as a total community—making sure to include those who prefer not to change anything—is a task that will challenge a group's keenest human relations skills and understandings. To enumerate the human resources needed for such a task is to risk oversimplification—but translated into daily human interaction, these resources are at the root of successful development of community when school change is necessary. And change is necessary if we are to meet the educational needs of students and improve the professional lives of teachers. Success at building a school community that is inclusive requires some careful change facilitation. Whether this facilitation is done by an outside facilitator, an inside facilitator, or a group who take on the task together, there are some essential skills that are necessary. The depth and productivity of the resulting collegial interaction is directly related to the skill of change facilitators. These are some of the specific skills that have proven to be important:

- knowledge of change theory,
- group dynamics skills, including knowledge of conflict resolution,
- knowledge of adult learning,
- knowledge of a variety of group decision-making structures,
- skill in seeing and acknowledging the positive contributions—however small—everyone makes,
- creating opportunities for many people to take on meaningful leadership roles, or use their skills and talents for the good of the community,
- genuine openness to the full spectrum of the school community,
- a thorough understanding of schools and schooling, along with the ability to encourage exploration of new possibilities in non-threatening ways,
- recognition of the need for balance in community work with

respect to visions, goals and objectives, action, and maintenance of personal interrelationships, and

- the ability to maintain perspective—to see the forest, not just the trees; to see the relationships among the interweaving and evolving processes of change.

Those who facilitate the school renewal effort must keep in mind these central questions:

- What are the patterns, habits, regularities of this particular school?
- What gets in the way of change?
- What encourages and sustains change?
- What are the situations in which this school already works together successfully as a community?
- Is there a new process or project where everyone might gain from working as a community?
- What's going on in the school lives of the teachers and students? What causes stress? What brings enjoyment? Can the stress be reduced, the enjoyment increased?
- How is communication? Does everyone know what is going on?
- What can be done to ensure that everyone is heard and everyone has a productive role? (Cooperative learning techniques are often fruitful.)
- How can differing views and conflict become opportunities for growth and learning?
- Why are changes being considered, and whose interests are being served?

Some realities that must be attended to in order to bring about successful community building and ongoing change and renewal are difficult, since they are realities not commonly addressed in schools where the focus is usually on goals and objectives that culminate in measurable action and concrete products. There is no formula for translating these areas into action since each community has its own character. Those nurturing the change process must do the translating for their particular setting.

- There are always double agendas in communities: cooperation for the good of the whole and protection of individual needs; process and product; feeling and thinking; reflection and action; content and affect. These dualities must be kept in balance.
- Trust, caring, affirmation, attention to feelings, and genuine empathy must be promoted continuously.
- There is no enemy camp—only people doing what they think is right. Affirming the necessity of dissent is essential. This means facilitators of change must work at not being defensive of their "baby." It also means acknowledging that those who do not want to change are an important factor for keeping the change zealots from dragging the whole establishment over the abyss in creative glee. It is important to give those who do not want to change a genuine place in the process: They are the control group; they provide the link to tradition; they are a focal point from which to reflect on why changes are being proposed and in whose interest the change is being enacted.
- Successful community interactions need celebration!
- People need to be kept aware of where they are in the change process. During this process members of a group may sometimes feel unsure, unclear, confused, threatened; they may want to retreat to the safety of old ways, want to take "time out," want to be left alone; they may feel angry, manipulated, even frightened. If these feelings are understood as a normal part of change, members of a group can usually support one another and weather these times. This is particularly true if opportunities are provided for individuals to vent their feelings, and if "old history" is taken care of. Sharing of these areas has to be done in a nonjudgmental atmosphere where constructive listening is the norm. Venting can become an excuse for doing nothing, however. Balance is again of great importance. Written or spoken reflections on the state of the process, what is being done well and what needs

attention, helps to maintain perspective. The use of metaphors is also helpful, such as the image of a pond freezing, unfreezing, and refreezing with all the various transmutations of ice in such a process. Someone needs to understand the dynamics of change. If no one does, it is important to get someone trained.

- Power is a factor. School-based change means an alteration of the traditional hierarchical power structure and can leave community members at all levels insecure. Teachers' power traditionally has been centered on autonomy behind classroom doors. To leave that power base for the uncertainty of shared power in a community setting is a big thing to ask of teachers. The good of the whole and collegial sharing can look unappealing if it threatens the security of the individual. That power shift must be treated with respect. Empowering teachers may be the newest "byword" in education, but the ramifications of that concept should not be treated lightly. It is not easy to change from a belief that power is finite and gets taken away from someone if given to others, to a belief that power is infinite and its diffusion increases the energy and creativity of the entire community. It is natural to cling to the power one has and avoid the risks of expanded power for all. Power is often viewed as a negative, a potential danger, rather than a source of vitality and creativity. To foster the notion that power is positive if used as shared creative energy rather than for control over others is a major challenge.
- Take care of your principal! As teachers become empowered, a principal's role shifts in ways that can be construed as a loss of power, rather than an expansion of power through inclusion. A principal is not an all-powerful, all-knowing person, and the role shift is critical. The principal experiences the same uncertainty, confusion, and vulnerability as anyone else.
- Majority rule as a basis for decision making may not be the most productive method for a community. Consensus, or some adaptation of it, merits exploration. Majority rule is based on winners and losers, creating a potential for factionalizing and for future sabotage. Consensus is based on all winners, which is an

159

encouragement for community.

- Change facilitators can lose objectivity. If that happens, it is important to acknowledge that loss and solicit leadership that can be objective.
- Balance time to work on both process and products. Process is sometimes seen as "wasting time," but it is the foundation of community as it addresses shared human concerns. The "products" or innovations will be ephemeral without the depth of humane process through which a change or innovation becomes institutionalized. Too many teachers have seen too many innovations come and go. Without a viable process for ongoing change and renewal, many more innovations will simply come and go.

At the outset of a school change and renewal process, the primary facilitators tend to orchestrate the essential interactions that promote the process or innovation. As their initiatives are successful, and as shared leadership and shared decision making become a reality within the community, their role should diminish. At this time, facilitators must have an understanding of community and of the shifts in the power structure this represents, including shifts in their own power role.

How the change facilitators handle their own role is critical to the endurance of change and renewal as an ongoing practice within the school community. Generally the facilitator role shifts from central figure to mentor, support person, and facilitator of others' leadership.

Some goals for a change facilitator wishing to encourage total school community in the change process have been identified:

- Work yourself out of a job.
- Foster shared decision making and expanded leadership.
- Develop group processes appropriate to the identified human and educational needs and the active projects underway.
- Teach others the skills for change facilitation you understand and use.

- Abdicate the position when someone within the school community can assume a change facilitator role. The more who can take on this role, the better for the community.
- Be a "cheerleader" for others' strengths and talents.
- Provide the resources others need to perform work for the good of the community—educational literature, appropriate consultants, time to talk.
- Be open about your own weak areas—acknowledge mistakes, insecurities, vulnerabilities—ask for help. Serving as role model for these fragile areas of community sharing is one of the most powerful things a change facilitator can do. It is a personal risk you cannot ask of others, if you cannot do it yourself.
- Resist the opportunity to play God. A competent change facilitator will have many opportunities for omnipotence. It can be a great relief to a community to find a savior, a guru, a rescuer, who can just as quickly become a scapegoat. A savior relieves people of personal responsibility and does not promote community, long-lasting change, or creative human interaction.
- Be scrupulously honest and honor confidences. Do not gossip or belittle anyone. If a change facilitator is not trusted by all, he or she cannot work effectively.
- Assist the adults in the community to keep in focus the knowledge that the lives and education of children are the raison d'etre for everything being done. It is the children who should constitute the motivating force of the school renewal community. However, that mission never precludes creating a healthy working environment for adults, since the texture of adults' lives directly affects the lives of students.

Change is a way of living in our age and will be integral to our future; it is said to be the only predictable constant. The lessons of change are hard to learn: Nothing is ever finished; making one significant change only leads to another, and another; it is a personal undertaking fraught with ambiguity. Change itself, with all its stresses and uncertainties, is an acquired taste, one that is not easy to develop in the face of our natural desire for stability and peace of mind. Nevertheless, the rewards of living creatively and exuberantly, and of sharing the joys of an open, honest, vital, and self-renewing community do compensate for the risks and responsibilities, the challenges of change.

11. THE PERSONAL AND THE INTERPERSONAL: NEGLECTED ASPECTS OF TEACHER LEADERSHIP

by Gary Rackliffe

On September 8, 1987, the staff of Adams Elementary School elected Rachel to chair the newly formed steering committee that would lead their participation in a school restructuring project. During the school's first year of participation, she kept a journal in which she described her reactions to this expansion of her role as a teacher, and this chapter is based on an analysis of that journal and interviews. All names, including the school's, have been changed to protect confidentiality.

School reform proposals for the professionalization of teaching include recommendations for teachers who have leadership roles in their schools. Although these proposals describe, in general terms, positions involving responsibilities for professional development, collegial interaction, and shared decision making, little is known about the personal reactions of teachers as they move into these positions. Rachel's journal provides insight into the meanings teacher leadership had for her as her school's renewal efforts began. These are important considerations for people interested in moving beyond the rhetoric of school improvement to actual changes in school practice.

RACHEL

Rachel has taught for 15 years, the last 13 in kindergarten. She also has teaching experience in second grade, first grade, pre-kindergarten, and compensatory reading. In addition to her bachelors degree in sociology and elementary education, she has completed a masters degree in early childhood teaching plus 30 additional hours. She has been married to a robotics engineer for 12 years, and they have no children.

Rachel was an early supporter of her school's reform effort, and was one of two or three people who were interested in chairing the steering committee. She said she was at a point in her career where she wanted to try something different, and this project seemed worth an investment of time and energy. She was chosen, with a large majority, by a vote of the steering committee in which she and one other person received votes.

ADAMS ELEMENTARY SCHOOL

Adams Elementary School is a neighborhood school with an enrollment of 385 students located in a city of over 150,000 people. In addition to kindergarten through fifth-grade classes, it has pre-kindergarten and a Pre-Primary Impaired program for three- to five-year-olds.

There are 15 classroom teachers at Adams; two Chapter I teachers, one each for reading and mathematics; and six aides. The building staff also includes a principal, secretary, instructional media center clerk, home-school counselor, and two custodians. Itinerant staff include specialists in reading and mathematics, social workers, speech therapists, a psychologist, an art and music team, and other consultants.

Collectively, the Adams faculty has accumulated 184 years of teaching experience. They have been at Adams for an average of 9.2 years, the most senior member having been in the building for 34 years while two teachers were in the building for the first year. Ninety percent of the professional staff have earned masters degrees, and the principal has a doctorate. The average age of the faculty is 42 years, and they range in age from 29 to 57.

The district in which Adams Elementary School is located is a leader in the community school concept. Students attend neighborhood schools unless bused to a magnet school. It was agreed from the outset that the school renewal project, as a community-wide effort, would reflect Adams' emphasis on community participation and its history of staff involvement. The steering committee has included members from all parts of the school staff and community members.

MEANINGS OF LEADERSHIP

The elements of what it meant for Rachel to be a teacher leader can be grouped into categories which are interwoven to form "leadership." I separate them in this analysis at the risk of giving a somewhat distorted view of the whole. Just as the examination of tasks performed by teachers can give us some sense of the nature of teaching, the examination of Rachel's perception of the components of leadership can give us some sense of what the role of teacher leader involves.

But these components can only be viewed as analytic categories whose existence is the result of an artificial deconstruction of the position of steering committee chair in this particular situation. The role is actually played out in the real world through an integration and interaction of all these elements, input from other players, and contextual factors that are only suggested here. In other words, this account is an oversimplification that might be helpful as we consider the establishment of expanded roles for teachers, but it is not, nor can it be, the whole story.

The categories presented here are interpersonal issues related to developing relationships with other people, and personal issues about herself and her personal and professional life. These are by no means clearly differentiated; each of them affects and interacts with the other, but they provide an opportunity to look at the social interactions of this position and the person filling it.

Dedication

Before considering Rachel's thoughts about leadership it will be helpful to look at her dedication to her school's renewal project, which underlies much of what is to follow. Rachel was one of the original supporters of the project, and when she became steering committee chair she saw supporting the project as a major part of that job. A number of times she commented in her journal about the importance

165

of the project and its potential for changing conditions at her school.

From time to time, however, she expressed doubts about whether the concept of teacher empowerment and shared decision making would work in Adams' situation. In her role as chair she was involved in discussions and activities that would boost her confidence in the project at one moment and then make her doubt the possibility of change the next moment. Throughout the experience, she felt she had to remain dedicated to the project and its philosophic base. During a period of tension in the fall she wrote in her journal, "This program offers us so much, I'm certainly not going to let animosity between us ruin it" (10/26/87).

Complicating this dedication, however, was the ambiguity of the project. There were no clear-cut guidelines laying out a procedure to follow. All the decisions were left to the school staff who often looked to Rachel for explanation or guidance. She referred to herself as the "person in the know" (10/29/87) and frequently talked to staff members about the benefits of the project which allowed them to set their own agenda for change.

INTERPERSONAL

Leadership in any endeavor is an interpersonal activity. In her journal Rachel wrote about four interpersonal aspects of leadership. The first two, developing new relationships and team building, are obvious and commonly found in other discussions of leadership. The second two, "can't please everyone" and being the center of attention, are somewhat more subtle.

Developing New Relations

Becoming a leader involved developing new or different relations with people Rachel had worked with for as many as 10 years. The design of the building aggravated the isolation teachers normally feel. Adams School has two wings that are connected at one end with the upper elementary grades in the B-wing and the primary grades in the A-wing. There is very little day-to-day contact between the teachers in

166

the different wings. As chair, Rachel came into contact and worked with people from both wings, and her relations with the principal and the district administration also changed.

Peers

Becoming better acquainted with other teachers was a benefit of Rachel's position. One day she wrote, "I had a surprising 'gift'—I got to know Roy better" (10/16/87). In interviews she often mentioned the value of learning about other teachers and their classrooms, as well as developing richer personal relationships with her peers.

However, the relationships that developed or changed were not all positive. Rachel also found she had to deal with conflict and disagreement differently than she had in the past. Before leading this project, she could go to her classroom and avoid conflict; now she was often at the center of it. During periods of conflict early in the project she and others learned to be "oh so civilized." When topics of strong disagreement were raised at meetings, Rachel had to make her points without becoming emotional or upset. Arguments were carried out peacefully, sometimes by talking to intermediaries, but the outward appearance was always civilized.

As time went on, Rachel, and the others, learned to focus on issues rather than personalities, although it was sometimes difficult to separate the two. She knew that as a leader she would have to avoid being drawn into personality conflicts. During a crisis period early in the year she "heard some flack about the meeting—general stuff. Tried to point out that we have to get beyond our personalities—me included—if this is going to work" (10/7/87). Progress toward this end was being made though, and in March she described a meeting by saying, "I was pleased at how far we have come. We are learning to sit and exchange ideas without getting personally involved. We are learning that it isn't necessary to win each point to establish our validity personally. A major step" (3/21-22/88).

Superiors

One project goal was to change the relationships between teachers and administrators by developing a more collegial atmosphere of shared decision making. Rachel realized that part of being a leader in this project would be learning new ways in which to relate to the building principal and to the district administration. She ended her first journal entry by saying, "Finally, I hope that Dr. Haslett [Adams principal] will accept me as chairperson—close work with him on a positive note will not only [be] helpful, but I also think necessary for the success of the program" (9/29/87).

The new relationship with the principal involved many hours of discussions in his office. These discussions became so common that one day Rachel said she would have to put her name on her regular chair. Conversations ranged from rambling philosophical discussions to what Rachel perceived to be heated debates over particular activities.

District policy requires teachers to communicate with the district administration through their building principal, so Rachel had few opportunities to contact administrators outside the building. The goal of the project does, however, extend to new relations with district administration, and Rachel wrote about the difficulty for all involved in changing existing patterns of interaction. "The problem with empowering elementary teachers is everyone is so used to telling us what to do, they don't know how to stop" (2/24/88). These patterns of behavior have developed over a number of years, and they will not change overnight.

Team Building

Rachel intuitively knew team building was an important part of being a leader. In her journal she wrote about five aspects of team building: communications, cheerleading, spreading ownership and sharing credit, compromising, and delegating.

Communications

Rachel had always been an active member of her faculty, but as a leader she found herself involved in many more conversations than ever before. "All I do is talk and run" (10/29/87). "At this morning's coffee, I never did get to sit down because every time I did, someone called to me to talk about this or that" (2/10/88). Because as steering committee chair Rachel represented the entire staff, some conversations put her in a position of listening to things with which she did not personally agree. "Maybe that's part of leadership—learning to talk and listen. Learning to do things that don't always feel right to you personally but are right when you look at the picture as a whole" (11/9-13/87).

Cheerleading

"I feel like the head cheerleader" (10/29/87). This aspect of leadership is closely related to Rachel's dedication. During public meetings and in private conversations Rachel acted as the project's head cheerleader. When people were uncertain about voting to participate in the project she encouraged them by explaining what she saw as the advantages.

Being cheerleader was not always an easy task. Upon her enthusiastic return from a restructuring conference, Rachel wrote, "I tried to talk to people—to give away a little of the energy/hope/ excitement, but not everyone is interested. So I held out a few carrots—sub bank—outside observations, conferencing time, etc. Got a little more interest" (10/13/87). Being cheerleader for a championship team with a loyal following is easier than being cheerleader for a team that is struggling to get started.

Spreading Ownership and Sharing Credit

These are widely recognized aspects of team building and leadership. One of the first events that made their importance explicit for Rachel was a talk by Ann Lieberman at a restructuring conference.

169

Lieberman discussed the importance of not creating closed groups within school staffs. Rachel wrote, "She talked about the realities of school reform—the inside/outside problems that affect it. So many of them applied to us, but, as she pointed out, they can be dealt with" (10/10/87).

Activities during the early months of the project were often complicated by tensions among groups within the staff, the problems Lieberman had warned about. As a part of building a team, Rachel had to work at not offending any of the groups. "I am trying to be real careful not to always be the one that blocks things—that way I don't alienate [any group]—oh politics" (10/28/87).

An example of sharing credit for project activities was a newspaper interview early in the project. A reporter for the local paper called the school and requested a phone interview about the project. "I felt since it was going to be quoted it was best to prepare a statement. So I started and then stood in the office and had everyone who would read it and comment" (10/27/87). When the reporter called her in the evening Rachel read the statement, "and I stressed repeatedly that it should be stressed that the statement, etc. was a cooperative effort and please stress this in the article" (10/27/87). When the article was published Rachel wrote that it was "not too bad—I thought it was pretty innocuous except my name is quoted so often" (10/30/87). The following Monday she wrote, "Not too many people mentioned it—don't know if they're upset. My name is the only one there—but I did try to tell the reporter to mention all of us" (11/2/87).

Compromising

It may be that compromise, which is implicit in much of what has been said, is the cornerstone that provides a foundation for this entire project. Rachel mentioned the need for compromise in a journal entry describing a rather heated meeting in the fall. The committee was debating who should represent the school in a presentation at a state-wide conference, and things did not go as Rachel would have wished. "I was a little upset [at the outcome] and that it should be a

170

group effort, but then I thought about it—I need to learn to compromise too. So I kept my mouth shut" (10/6/87).

Delegating

A final feature of team building that Rachel mentioned was sharing responsibility with others, both in terms of asking others to do things and trusting them to follow through. This feature became more of an issue as committees were formed and began working independently. "This new phase of the project is going to be the hardest for me. I have to learn to let go and to trust others. I have to stop thinking that things won't get done if I'm not involved. I am not indispensable, and I want to make myself realize this" (2/15/88). There were a number of situations in which Rachel had to learn to live with things the way others did them rather than trying to do everything herself.

Can't Please Everyone

A harder lesson to learn about team building is that it does not always work, and you have to accept that some people will not be pleased. This lesson was difficult to accept because it contradicted much of what she was doing in terms of team building and cheerleading. In the early days of the project a number of confrontations occurred, and after one of these she wrote,

> The interesting thing was I didn't feel panic—I just thought, "Oh well, not everyone can be happy." This is a real switch for me—normally I feel obligated to please everyone, and, even though that's impossible, I tear myself up trying. In the past Dr. Haslett has on a number of times reminded me of that—to no avail. But, now I seem to be changing whether that's good, I don't know, but changing I am. He's right—you can't please everyone (10/13/87).

This lesson, like some others, Rachel seemed to be learning a number of times. In December, just after the state-level conference, when things were relatively settled, she was refining this idea of

171

pleasing everyone to include the idea that you cannot do everything for everyone. She wrote,

> I also feel my attitude changing. I [am] beginning to realize you can't please everyone, and you don't have to. . . . This attitude has come out of the conference—you can only do so much and then you just move on. I've spent my life bending over backwards for others and finally at 35 I'm learning it's only necessary to bend so far, then it's OK to stand up (12/16/87).

Psychic Rewards

There was, however, a contrasting side to leadership for Rachel. It wasn't always team building and sharing credit; it also involved being at the center of activity and attention. These ego-boosts were part of the pay-off for the work she did. There was often a tension or actual conflict between Rachel's desire to promote the group and her enjoyment of the attention that came with the position of chair. She wrote about this in terms of power relations and being at the center of attention.

Power

During an early crisis Rachel had to insist on changes being made in the names appearing on the printed program for a state-level conference the steering committee had been invited to address. A number of phone calls were made, there was a confrontation, and at the last minute the changes were made. After the incident she wrote,

> How did I feel—triumphant. I got through to him—finally! Also a little powerful. I see it in little ways—how I word a note, how I react to others, how I feel about myself. Do I like it—I think so, but I think I'll reserve comment or commitment for now" (11/3/87).

After other confrontations during the year this feeling of having the power to make things happen increased, and Rachel appreciated it as a tool to use in moving toward the project's goals.

Center of Attention

For a classroom teacher who had become accustomed to spending all of her professional life with kindergarten students or, for a few days each year, in inservice activities being told how to do her job, being steering committee chair for a national project moved Rachel into situations that were new to her. It was a new experience to be treated like a celebrity. At the state-wide conference where the steering committee presented at one session, she wrote,

What was nice was the recognition we got—and I enjoy it. Everyone— . . . Jack [the local teachers' association president], Alice Anderson [state vice president] was very solicitous. I think it sunk into Roy's head just how important we are—the attention we got when we walked in, the attention we got at lunch—we sat next to the head table . . . being mentioned in Alice Anderson's speech, being mentioned [by] the [national] director who was the keynote speaker. Roy finally looked at me and said we must be important. I said we sure are! (12/11/87).

The next day she wrote,

What is happening to me? I am actually enjoying the limelight, and I guess—can this be true—I want it. This is a side of myself I have trouble recognizing and accepting. I'll have to think about this a while—can I handle leading—I think I can (12/12/87).

Rachel enjoyed the attention associated with the newspaper interview mentioned above, and she understood the value to the project of sharing the credit. On the other hand, she also felt a need for personal recognition. After the phone call from the reporter she wrote, "I also have developed a new attitude—since I'm working very hard at this—I want a little recognition. Is this a power trip??? I think not—more a justification for spending my life currently on this project!!" (10/27/87)

173

PERSONAL

In her journal Rachel often exposed very private feelings about the meanings leadership had for the personal side of her life. In a conversation about my analysis of her journal, she said she had been surprised at her candor when she was writing. She considers herself a relatively private person who, although quite social, is slow to share personal feelings with others. She wrote entries in her journal for more than two months before showing them to me. During this period especially, and throughout the year to a lesser degree, she viewed the journal more as a private diary than as research data to be examined, analyzed, and reported. With this private, almost confidential, nature in mind, I would like to discuss the personal aspects of her leadership. Rachel and I agreed at the outset of the project, and again in later conversations, that it is important to discuss these issues and make them a part of a complete understanding of what being a leader meant to her.

In this February journal entry Rachel wrote about many of the personal issues. It is obvious that these issues are intertwined both among themselves and with the broader, public issues discussed above.

You asked why I'm burned out—I guess I'm just tired. It's been a long year and not just from the project. Being over limit in my classroom last fall, trying to break in a new teacher now, fighting the feeling of isolation I feel because I'm always running off to meetings and I have no time for my friends, feeling the constant demands on my time by other people—it's all wearing on me. Yes, I can admit, people's attitudes towards me have changed—I feel they're always waiting for me to find the solution, for me to get through to Dr. Haslett, for me to have the time to listen. I guess that's what everyone wants a teacher leader to be there for, unfortunately, I also have to teach full time, and I feel this need to be even better at that than usual to prove I can do both jobs without shorting either one (2/29/88).

The interpersonal aspects of leadership were generally played out on a public stage, but the personal aspects of leadership were private and seen by a much smaller audience, if by anyone at all. The first of these was Rachel's personal commitment to her professional responsibility as a kindergarten teacher. Finally, there are issues of loneliness, isolation, and self-denial that were part of being a leader.

Super Teacher

The first personal decision Rachel made was to not allow the work of steering committee chair to infringe on her responsibility to her students. In her third journal entry she wrote, "I am determined to be Super Teacher—give my best to the kids and still be able to handle this" (10/1/87). Later in the month as more people were making more demands on her time she wrote, "I am determined that I'll be an even better teacher to prove this can be done without sacrificing the kids. I sometimes wonder if it's an impossible dream. If I can just get by report cards I'll be home free—at least I hope I will be" (10/29/87). Unfortunately, she was not home free, and the demands on her time and energy continued to make her dedication to her students difficult.

In the spring, as a way of providing more time for teachers, committees started using release days for meetings. Getting substitute teachers for half- or whole-day sessions had the advantage of allowing longer blocks of time during which teachers could consider more complex issues, but it also meant more time out of the classroom for Rachel and other teachers. Because of the number of committees Rachel was involved with she was taken out of her room more often than other teachers, which concerned her and was a major reason for her cutting back on committee memberships in the spring.

Friends

Another aspect was the way in which the demands on Rachel's time and emotional energy cut her off from her friends. Many lunch periods, which had been social occasions, were now devoted to committee meetings, a change that bothered Rachel, as can be seen in the following entry.

Today, I don't know what my problem was—I guess I was playing hookie—meetinged out. I guess I just figured it would all come together on its own. I guess I needed to touch base with people outside of [the project]. I have begun to feel isolated from some of my friends— and I'm not alone—they make comments to me about never seeing me anymore. And so I needed to squeeze some time in for Christine (1/12/88).

Self-denial

The topic of self-denial appears often as Rachel, in a number of ways, deemphasized her needs for what she saw as the good of the group. The resulting tension often led to physical reactions as demonstrated by this entry: "The business of always having to worry about others' feelings and others' reactions forces you to put your own to one side. It also causes you to doubt your own decisions. It also causes you to resume drinking Maalox and eating aspirin" (11/9-13/87). Other times she wrote of being forced by her position to restrain herself. After a particularly trying confrontation with a friend Rachel wrote, "All I really wanted to do was scream at her, 'You think you're under pressure??? What about me!' but I can't do that because people expect me to persevere" (4/27/88).

CONCLUSION

This study has offered a look at Rachel, who is typical—at least not atypical—of teachers in restructuring endeavors who move into expanded roles that take them out of their classrooms and into situations involving other adults. It has provided some insights into aspects of that role expansion which have implications for schools and individuals who want to change the nature of teachers' jobs by increasing shared decision making and collegial interaction.

Those insights suggest that schools should do better than create new situations and roles in which teachers must simply persevere. Broad-range, lasting improvement in the outcomes of schooling will not come about through minor adjustments in our traditional methods of schooling. Restructuring calls for significant changes in

176

the nature of teachers' work, both in terms of their relations with others in the school building and in the ways people outside the building view their work. Through her journal Rachel has shown us that these changes cannot be brought about by decree, and that the setting in which they occur must provide thoughtful consideration for the people who are expected to make such changes in the long-term patterns of their personal and professional lives.

12. DEFINING A LEGITIMATE ROLE FOR STUDENTS AS PARTNERS IN EDUCATION REFORM

by Terry Mazany

Embedded within education-driven school reform is an inherent contradiction that renders many such efforts ineffective and, in fact, may prevent the achievement of the fundamental goals of educational improvement and human enrichment. On the one hand, education reform has borrowed the notion that persons affected by a decision should have input into that decision. On the other hand, the prevalent bias in our traditional approach to education is to define students as passive receivers of knowledge. These views cannot co-exist. If education reform is to succeed, our definition of the role of the student in the education process must change at the onset of reform.

A MORE COMPLETE DEFINITION OF EDUCATION REFORM

A major subset of approaches to education reform involves the structural redesign of organizational management processes. Current models have either built on pioneering work in business or government, or they represent cases of independent, but parallel, invention. All of these models can be classified according to three basic dimensions:

- *Empowerment.* Delegating decision-making authority to the school, the principal, the teachers, or some other position. Empowerment represents a vertical push of decision making downward in the organization.
- *Shared Decision Making.* Opening channels for involvement in decision making outward or horizontally within the organiza-

179

tion. Shared decision making implies increasing access to, and input in, decision making, but not a sharing or delegating of the authority to make decisions.

- *Planning.* A proactive response to change that involves the need to restructure and redefine instructional time to accommodate this activity—otherwise this activity is carried out by staff offices.

Each component can be instituted independent of the others, but all three components must be incorporated in order to realize the full measure of potential benefits of reform.

STUDENTS AS LEGITIMATE STAKEHOLDERS

Proceeding from the assumption that persons affected by a decision must have input into that decision, the basic design imperatives for education reform require revision. An analysis of the school as the basic unit of change indicates the existence of at least five primary stakeholders: students, parents/community, non-instructional staff, instructional staff, and administration. The optimal design of school reform would include all five stakeholders in the basic partnership for reform.

The inclusion of teachers in reform projects is a natural first step, and may be an essential step prior to the inclusion of the other stakeholders. Student involvement, on the other hand, is more problematic. First, teachers must experience sufficient control over their work to feel secure and empowered to initiate change in the classroom. Second, parents must be informed and supportive of new approaches to classroom learning and management practices.

In addition, specific mindsets defining students in our schools and society may need to be changed. These mindsets include the belief that students are not interested in learning, that students must be controlled, and that student-initiated ideas are a challenge to adult authority and infallibility (leading to a loss of control and the unraveling of the entire social framework on which a school depends—thus student involvement will be seen by some as a high-risk proposition).

STUDENT RIGHTS IN THE DESIGN
OF EDUCATION REFORM

If participants in a reform project determine initially that student involvement will enhance their efforts, the design of that involvement requires serious consideration to ensure that the students can successfully carry out their roles in the project. It is not sufficient to grant students rights to membership in the reform process. They must be accorded the full set of rights granted the other stakeholders; namely, the right of representation, the right of assembly, the right of veto, and the right to mutual respect.

Students must have the right to select their own representatives; those representatives must have the right to meet with their constituents; and they must have veto rights equal to the other parties in the shared decision-making process. Finally, they must be accorded equal respect by virtue of being fellow human beings, and not treated as second-class citizens whose voices do not count because they are "kids" or are "there to learn, and not to tell adults what to do."

The involvement of students in a project also requires support from adult participants in terms of both patience and the freedom to fail. Students, accustomed to being controlled, will require months—if not years—to assert self-control. As they progress through this transition, they will make mistakes. The adults play a critical role in supporting mistake making and the ability to learn from mistakes.

REDEFINING STUDENT LEADERSHIP

Education reform and student participation in that reform is hindered by a traditional view of leadership. This model defines the ideal leader as either a paternalistic, take-charge person who has all the answers and is infallible, or as a maternal guardian who protects but creates dependency. These models can account for a significant proportion of the leadership behavior displayed by classroom teachers and school principals. The negative consequences of these styles are that they create dependency and disempower those being led. Followers of such leaders assume no responsibility for the actions and outcomes in their lives.

Over the past two decades a new model of leadership has emerged within our society and particularly within the context of participative management. This model is better suited for participatory approaches to decision making, and is, in fact, essential for the successful institutionalization of participative management. This "empowering leader" is one who follows the Lao Tzu dictum, "The best of all leaders is the one who helps people so that eventually they don't need him." The very nature of shared decision making demands this style of leadership, and the goals of education improvement and human enrichment can best be furthered in this manner.

WHAT DOES THIS LEGITIMATE ROLE LOOK LIKE?

The legitimization of the role of students as partners in education reform requires both the commitment to grant students the same rights accorded to the other partners and the initiation of support practices within the schools to guarantee these rights. These supportive practices include:

- the school's commitment to student leadership and rights as a priority, including recruiting the best teachers for sponsorship, gaining school-wide support for this activity from the entire faculty, converting student government into a regularly scheduled class, and supplying student government with the resources required to bring about school improvement;
- a curriculum for all students that includes development of the qualities of good student leadership and representation;
- student government practices based on win/win negotiation techniques and consensus building, instead of the win/lose strategies of parliamentary procedure;
- the use of cooperative learning strategies in the classroom;
- skills training in the homeroom setting for conflict resolution,

facilitation, effective meetings, problem solving, consensus, and presentation techniques; and

- involvement of the parents of student leaders so that support for these changes and activities is better understood and broadened.

THE BOTTOM LINE: SOCIAL AND HUMAN ENRICHMENT

Three primary benefits emerge from this restructuring of the process of education reform. First, this approach enriches the education process for the students, who can acquire increased self-esteem and an attitude of empowerment. Second, this approach creates a better fit between the student and the society, and the student and the work he or she will undertake in the future. Finally, this approach provides a better opportunity to develop leadership capable of meeting the challenges of the future.

Experience in the private and public sectors can bring clarity to the means and ends of education reform. A basic policy goal for worker involvement has been the enhancement of human dignity and the enrichment of society by reconciling the practices of the workplace with the values of our democracy.

Experience has shown that change reaching into the work site requires at least five to ten years of an organization's involvement. We in education cannot afford to replicate models that require that many years for the impact to be felt in the classroom. Our challenge is to experiment with the known and take risks with the unknown to pioneer reform that reaches directly into the classroom and empowers young people so that they become true partners in their education.

13. ENLISTING PARENTS AS PARTNERS IN SCHOOLING

by Dorothy C. Massie

Home is a child's first school; the parent is the child's first teacher; reading is the child's first subject.

—Barbara Bush, March 10, 1989

Parental involvement in education is in danger of becoming, like the traditional American family, one of the great American cliches—honored rhetorically, remembered nostalgically, but more often idealized than realized.

In many communities across the nation, the bonds between schools and families have been strained beyond the breaking point for a complex mixture of reasons: urbanization; changes in family structure; the conflicts of school desegregation; immigration, which has diversified the cultures and ethnicity of many schools; the flight from public schools and cities of many middle- and upper-middle class families; and the technological changes that have diminished the role of schools in the lives of American children and their parents.

Although these forces have tended to alienate families from public schools, it is encouraging to note countering trends.

As the effects of the recent wave of state-led school reform measures trickled downward during the 1980's—bringing pressures for more accountability, more testing, and a more rigidly "back-to-basics" curriculum—some very different kinds of education reform have been percolating upward, from local schools, university child study centers, and citizens' groups.

This quieter school reform movement seeks to accomplish its goal—making schools work better for all youngsters—by bridging the gap between schools and families.

Here are examples of efforts to involve parents meaningfully in the education of their children:

- Once a week, in Donaldsonville, Louisiana, a school bus takes from 30 to 40 young mothers and two fathers, to a local elementary school where they spend the morning learning how to "make book-reading fun" for their kids. Taking turns during the first hour, parents read aloud to their first-grade children and are critiqued by the group. In the second hour, they view videotapes of the previous week's efforts and join in a discussion of techniques for reading aloud. Identified as "Parents as Partners," the program's objective is to improve the literacy rate among socioeconomically deprived families by teaching parents how to read aloud to their children (Maraniss 1989).
- In Missouri, an innovative early childhood program, "Parents as Teachers," educates parents of children under age three on various facets of a child's growth—language, curiosity, and social and learning skills—to help parents enhance their children's development and detect health or other problems early enough for successful intervention. Results of the program's three-year pilot phase completed in 1984 showed that on tests for intelligence, language ability, and school-related success, children in the program scored higher than their peers.
- In Maryland, a program with the acronym TIPs—Teachers Involve Parents—introduces teachers to components of parent involvement projects that extend the boundaries of the school curriculum in remedial instruction, review, practice, completion of school work, or enrichment. (Epstein 1985).
- A parent participation program initiated in 1968 in two of the poorest, most chaotic schools of inner-city New Haven succeeded in transforming them into two of the city's highest achieving schools. Today, more than 20 years later, the essential elements of the program are being introduced in all New Haven Public Schools and are being used in more than 50 schools around the country. Directed by James Comer of Yale University's Child Study Center, the program involves parents at

186

three levels in the schooling of their children: as participants in a broad array of school activities; as volunteer aides in the classroom; and in school governance through the election of parent members to a school management team (Comer 1988).

- In Twin Falls, Idaho, the National Committee for Citizens in Education is working with parents of Headstart children, helping them make the transition from Headstart to public schools. The program offers information on parents' rights and training in the skills that will enable them to interact more effectively with the schools.

- At Spring Creek Elementary School, in Chattanooga, Tennessee, a Parent Involvement Program provides many different ways of communicating with parents, encouraging them to assist and evaluate their children's work at home. One parent was so challenged by her involvement with the program that she returned to school and completed her GED.

DIFFERING STRATEGIES, DIFFERING OPINIONS

Reflecting the trends toward an enlivened school-family interaction has been the reincarnation of the National Coalition for Parent Involvement in Education. This umbrella group of 30 national organizations, established in the late 1970's, was dissolved in 1982, but is once again an active school-community force.

B. J. Yentzer (1989) of the National Education Association, coalition president, commented, "There is no debate about the value of connecting families with their children's education. Research has demonstrated this beyond question. Where we are now is at the point of finding ways to do that most effectively."

Of the different ways to achieve parent-school cooperation, Nancy Berla (1989) of the National Committee for Citizens in Education said,

All parents should be involved one way or another, either at home

187

or in the school room, at some level, in the education of their children; there is no one best method for this. Even for parents who both work, or single parents, there still are things that can be done—working with the child at home, going in when there's a problem. But the principal has to set the tone and say that this is important. If he or she doesn't, then teachers who do not find it easy to interact with parents will not involve them.

Among the ways schools are reaching out to their communities are:

Through community relations: providing school facilities as resources to the community, making the school a community center, and using the community—its institutions, businesses, families—as a resource to the school.

Public relations, public information: maintaining a systematic program of communication, through the media and through school-produced publications to acquaint the community with the accomplishments and needs of the schools.

Parent involvement: in several ways, nominally or meaningfully. For example, parents' participation in school activities may be:

- *Through parental governance or advisory committees and boards* in policy-setting, shaping of curriculum, and selection of texts and library materials. This may be a token arrangement, of little use to anyone, or a substantive one, as has existed in some Title I Parent Advisory Boards, and in the Yale-New Haven school intervention project. These programs have produced significant academic gains, reduced student absenteeism and behavior problems, and eliminated some of the mistrust and stereotypes that have separated schools from families—particularly poor and minority families, who have had little reason to trust America's institutions.
- *In organizations to promote school interests* through fund-raising, social events, and school-community liaison activities. Parent-Teacher Associations serve these functions admirably in many communities, and the National PTA is an important voice for education throughout the country.

- *As volunteers and paid aides in schools and classrooms.* The Yale-New Haven project initially provided for Title I-funded teacher aides in every classroom. Discussing this feature of the project, Comer (1988) recalled that children of nonparticipating parents identified with and used as parent surrogates the parent aides in the school.
- *Through regular school-home communications.* For example, the Parent Involvement Program at Spring Creek Elementary School includes a systematic exchange of information with parents: assignment sheets sent home each day to be checked by parents; weekly homework sheets to be returned, signed by the parents; and weekly progress reports and homework sheets sent to first-grade parents every Monday, including activities in which parents must be involved. Some schools use newsletters and recorded telephone messages to tell parents what their children are studying at school and how they can help. Parent-teacher conferences are, of course, one of the most widely used methods of teacher-parent two-way communication.
- *Through tutoring and assisting children at home.* Joyce Epstein of Johns Hopkins University, developer of the TIPs materials, with Henry Jay Becker, conducted an extensive survey of teachers and parents in 600 Maryland schools, finding that of all the types of parent involvement, parental supervision and assistance of children at home is the most educationally significant (Epstein 1984).

Specific kinds of assistance at home include reading aloud to children; having them read to parents; encouraging home discussions; watching together and discussing selected television programs, perhaps using school discussion guides; playing family games; conducting simple science experiments; going to the library together; and using school materials on a loan basis. Mt. Vernon School in Alexandria, Virginia, has a resource room where parents can work with their children and borrow materials to use at home.

A superb source of information and insights on "teachable

moments" for parents and their children is the book, *Megaskills: How Families Can Help Children Succeed in School and Beyond* by Dorothy Rich (1988), Director of the Home and School Institute in Washington, D.C. Megaskills, Rich writes, are those "superbasics"— confidence, motivation, effort, responsibility, initiative, caring, common sense, teamwork, and problem-solving—qualities essential for success in school and life that can be nurtured (or stifled) at home.

A CONSENSUS ON ESSENTIALS

Different methods of involving parents in education may work best for different school environments and grade levels. But whatever methods are used, the essential components of working successfully with parents, all action researchers seem to agree, include clear goals for each program; adequate and appropriate training of teachers to work effectively with parents; careful training of parents who will be involved as tutors, aides, school-home liaison workers, or in other roles; and, of overall importance, a school principal committed to the program of parent involvement.

Tom Schultz (1989) of the Association of State Boards of Education has confirmed further the consensus of current research on parent involvement:

> For too long we've taken a cosmetic approach to parental involvement. I think there's been a tendency to say, "Family structures are changing—with mounting divorce rates, the proliferation of one-parent families, problems of poverty, teen-age parents—and isn't all that just too bad? It's not our fault, and we can't expect these families to be involved in their children's education as families were involved back in the 50's."
>
> We've known for quite awhile that parent involvement is an important component of the education of children. An overarching need, if we are going to be serious about this, is to provide the resources to sustain it on a regular basis, to provide staff training for working with parents, and to build parent involvement programs into the work schedules of regular teachers.

REFERENCES

Berla, N. 1989. Telephone interview with author, February 1989.

Comer, J. P. 1988. Educating poor minority children. *Scientific American* 259 (5): 42-48.

Epstein, J. 1984. Testimony presented to the select committee on children, youth and families. Washington, D.C.: June 7, 1984.

Epstein, J. 1985. From research to practice: developing TIPs (teachers involve parents). Paper presented at American Educational Research Association Annual Meeting, Chicago.

Maraniss, D. 1989. Storybook success in literacy: Program helps parents read to children. *The Washington Post.* February 21, 1989: pp. 1,6.

Rich, D. 1988. *MegaSkills: How families can help children succeed in school and beyond.* Boston: Houghton Mifflin.

Schultz, T. 1989. Telephone interview with author, February 1989.

Yentzer, B. J. 1989 Telephone interview with author, February 1989.

AFTERWORD

LEARNING COMMUNITIES: REFLECTIONS ON OUR WORK

by Gary A. Griffin

FROM ISOLATION TO COMMUNITY

Faculty-led, school-based renewal has helped people in schools move from institutionalized isolation to ongoing dialogue. The isolation has not only separated teachers from teachers; it has separated schools from schools, ideas from ideas, theories from theories, practices from theories. Renewal is recreating an interactive, ongoing community of interests, not just providing opportunities for people to interact.

Some may say, "All they're doing is getting together more." No, we are not simply getting together as human beings. Our ideas are getting together, our schools and our practices are getting together, and this is creating a rich mix of human and intellectual resources.

In the 1960's, John Goodlad led a major study of school change. In the study, they discovered one process that endured and was associated with successful school change—DDAE, standing for Dialogue, Decision Making, Action, and Evaluation. It wasn't pretty, it wasn't neat and clean, but it was always there in schools that were making differences. DDAE was in the center of successful change and, importantly, it recycled itself as new changes were encountered and implemented (Bentzen 1974). The new communities of learners that have emerged as a result of faculty-led renewal are recreating the possibilities discovered in DDAE.

We are going from believing that only children and teachers are school learners, to understanding that everyone in the school is a learner—demonstrating the practices of a community of learners and demonstrating that learners in schools find that the process of learning is exciting, frustrating, tension-ridden. It is also incomplete and unending.

Consider this statement by Colonel Francis Parker (1897): "I began to keep school 42 years ago. I began to learn how to teach some 25 years ago, and today I feel deeply that I have not yet learned the fundamental principles of education."

We can recognize, comfortably and positively, that we have not yet mastered the fundamentals of education, but we must be willing to continue investigating.

FROM ISOLATED IDEAS TO SHARED VISIONS

Faculties are moving from multiple, isolated, and private educational visions to shared, core views as they grapple with the creation of a central set of beliefs that will guide their work together. That's very different from business as usual. It is most unusual to see people within schools, and much less across schools, go from these isolated, disparate, unconnected views about education to shared visions.

FROM UNITARY TO SHARED LEADERSHIP

We are learning what it takes to go from a single, designated instructional leader to shared leadership. We know that the single leader model has never been effective because it suggests an impossible job. The modern exigencies of just "keeping school" make it impossible. We must think of ways to share leadership. The interesting thing about this new way of thinking about leadership is that it is based in large measure on choice, interest, and expertise. I am confident that the third component, expertise, will develop as teachers are drawn into the decision-making process.

FROM CONFORMITY TO CREATIVITY

We are also moving from conformity to external standards, requirements, rules, and regulations, to experimentation, creation, and invention. That is tough. Few of us have been encouraged to experiment, to create, and to invent. As a result, we are often uneasy about moving away from conformity, not from an unwillingness to create, invent, and experiment, but from a lack of opportunity, a lack of expertise, and a form of self-doubt.

Remember what Frances Fuller (Fuller and Bown 1975) found in her research? She noted that teachers generally move through three major stages of concern. The first is self: Am I good enough? Smart enough? Adequate? Will the kids like me? Will the principal approve of me? Will the parents want their children in my class? Am I good enough?

When these self-conscious concerns are settled, we teachers become concerned with task: Can I do the job? Can I get the papers distributed? Will the class activities move smoothly? Can I accomplish the tasks of teaching?

The third stage of concerns is impact: So what? Is what I'm doing well making a difference for students?

Faculty-led school renewal invites all of these stages at once. We are probably in this work primarily because we are asking the "so what?" question. Am I making a difference? As we ask that, and begin to experiment, invent, try out, we run right back to self-concerns: Can I do that? Am I clever enough? Am I convincing enough? Am I thoughtful enough?

In any group of teachers engaged in this process, we could expect to find some people self-conscious about their work, others in the process of mastering renewal tasks, and still others already saying, "Okay, we know. We've been through this before. So what? Is it making any real difference for us, for the kids?"

FROM WALLS-UP BUNKERISM
TO IDEAS SHARING

Faculties engaged in school renewal are also going from what I call institutional bunkerism (all the walls are up) to sharing practical, theoretical, research, and craft ideas. Again, that is unusual in American schools.

We researchers live in a wonderful world. We engage in what I call the "rape and pillage" of elementary and secondary schools. We move in and drop our student teachers and pick them up 18 weeks later. Or, we come in and gather test score data that we analyze in our own offices. Then what do we do? We talk to each other: "Say, Researcher A, this is Researcher B. What did you find out about effective teachers?" "Well, I found out that they do this." "Oh, that's terrific." Then we write it all up in a language only we can decipher. (It is claimed that there is one person who understands all the language of research. I don't know who that is.)

But the point is that we don't have good connections that help us to recreate our shared research and practice worlds with one another. The key here is sharing. There is knowledge and skill aplenty in both environments. We must continue to build bridges between research and practice, bridges created of shared meaning, mutual concerns, and equal investment in problem solving.

THE INTELLECTUAL DIMENSIONS
OF OUR CRAFT

I'd like to see people giving more attention to the academic disciplines, how they are changing, and how those changes are relevant to school subjects. I'd like to see educators thinking about schools as social organizations, human organizations. It is in these organizations that the changes in our world will be seen in the forms of content. We must not focus only on such abstract conceptions as "leadership." We must also focus on the content of our teaching, whether mathematics, social or physical sciences, whatever.

I'd like to see school-based study groups critiquing and reviewing, not just accepting, the research literature on teaching, schooling, learning, curriculum.

Teaching is a deeply intellectual activity. We make all kinds of decisions as teachers. This is the work of the mind. Even when we're deciding to move a student because s/he's talking to a neighbor, a kind of practical decision, we are engaging in intellectual activity that should be soundly informed by knowledge. It may be good for that child to talk to the neighbor. On what grounds do we decide to change the seat assignment or not?

I'd like to see us examine our own hearts and souls and ask, "What are the intellectual dimensions of teaching, and how can we strengthen them through school renewal?"

We must focus on the school as it is nested in the larger society and remain sensitive to the problems and tensions and dilemmas and changes of that society. We must link our work in schools to the features of this larger culture which they serve. We are not islands in the storm. In some measure, we are the storm. We must understand that.

There was a wonderful book title years ago: *Dare the Schools Build a New Social Order?* (Counts 1932). Some of us say, "Yes, the schools should dare to build a new social order." At the least, though, most of us would say, "Yes, the schools should be responsive to, and understanding of, the social order."

CHANGE, RESISTANCE, NEGOTIATED SHARING

Another thing I hope we can do is expect the tensions, expect the conflicts that come with change. These are natural phenomena associated with true change. They are to be expected; not something we should allow to halt our dialogue. When a central office, or even some of our own colleagues, give us trouble, we must understand that as an expected phenomenon. Change is not smooth sailing.

One way to approach resistance is to get smart about how adults learn and change. For the first time in our history, we are beginning to develop a major body of knowledge about how adults learn and change. If we understand that knowledge as we encounter resistance, we may just be smart enough to translate the knowledge into opportunities for those who oppose us to join us. The point is that a little learning may go a long way in terms of changing a resister to an ally.

Remember something else: Shared decision making is just that—shared. It is not taking decision making away from someone, it is sharing. We must begin to work with people, understand how they will learn and change, and become intrigued with what they are doing. This can happen because we are willing to share and compromise, not in negative ways, but compromise in order to negotiate the sharing of authority.

LANGUAGE MATTERS

The issue of language is still a problem. Discussions of school restructuring continue to generate a lot of loose usage of language. It is clear that people often are not talking about the same thing although they are using the same words. The redefinition and refinement of the language of practice, of change, of innovation, of possibility is best accomplished by teachers actively and thoughtfully involved in the process.

The meaningless usage of language gets in our way. Using words that don't say what they mean, or obscure meaning, or don't mean anything at all ends up in the trading of meaningless assertions and meaningless assents. One way to keep ourselves and one another honest is to keep our language honest.

PARADIGMS AND PATIENCE

Although there is much discussion of the way paradigms constrain our thinking and our envisioning, we must remember as we forge fresh ones that paradigms also can be helpful. Paradigms help us to create communities of interest. Paradigms link us through shared values and shared expectations. Paradigms lead us to be disposed to act together as opposed to acting separately. Paradigms often help us to formulate, and make public, intellectual and social identities. As we become entranced with "cracking" paradigms, as we become paradigm pioneers, and as we try to emulate what's going on in the corporate world, we also should remember that in social service organizations that have some relationship to the public good, paradigms need not

200

always be negative.

Amatai Etzioni used a wonderful phrase when he talked about organizations and changing them. When attempting to alter organization character, mission, outcomes, productivity, nature, he cautions us with the slogan: "Gradualism versus grandeur." Given the choice, go more gradually than grandly. So many of us are caught up in so many activities, events, and ways of thinking which may be in competition with one another, not just for time and energy, but because the activities and events themselves are competitive. They may not be complementary or mutually beneficial. When you get caught up in 9,000 projects, remember, "Gradualism versus grandeur."

MUTUAL ADAPTATION

Berman and McLaughlin (1975) conducted a major study of school change, in the course of which they invented a wonderful phrase, "mutual adaptation." This notion means that an innovation or change that comes into contact with people and places will change, as will the places and people. All change, all adapt.

Sometimes I hear those who are dissatisfied with the effects of their work say, "It didn't go quite like we had planned it." The fidelity was not 100 percent. So what? Examine what has happened and ask if the power of the context was such that we should expect the innovation itself to change in the same way that the context was expected to change. Keep "mutual adaptation" as a beacon. It can be very comforting when things don't go exactly as planned.

THE EXTENDED FAMILY OF LEARNING

We must go beyond the notion of the learning community as being composed of teachers and kids to include parents, community leaders, business and industry leaders, and other people in the education business.

We must continue to link everything we do to the improvement of educational opportunity for children and youth. I urge this for social, moral, and ethical reasons, as well as frankly political reasons.

201

We must make faculty-led school renewal a welcoming, invitational enterprise. Avoid implicit or explicit exclusion. Remember the lesson of the 1960's and 70's when model schools were selected to be beacons of change. These models or beacons or lighthouses eventually became isolated outposts, unconnected to the rest of the world. They served no useful purpose for other schools or other systems of education and, eventually, they either atrophied and died or had to be cut out because of their exotic and unfamiliar, threatening natures. We must avoid these consequences, which we can accomplish in some measure by being invitational and welcoming to others concerned about our work.

AND NOW?

My remarks have focused attention on the ways we think about our work and how our thinking influences our colleagues, our patrons, and our students. In familiar ways, this preoccupation with thinking pushes us to consider ideas and recommendations from the familiar education-oriented academic disciplines: sociology, psychology, philosophy, history, and the like.

Let's not forget the importance for our work of poets, writers, artists. The imagined world is worth considering, too. For example, as we continue in our quest for altering the conditions of teaching and learning in our schools, we may want to heed the words of the narrator in *The Moviegoer,* who says, "The search is what anyone would undertake if he were not sunk in the everydayness of his own life. . . . To become aware of the possibility of the search is to be onto something. Not to be onto something is to be in despair" (Percy 1979, p. 13).

We're onto something. We are fully engaged with the search for possibility. We are changing our own "everydayness." What's next? Let's find out together.

REFERENCES

Bentzen, M.M. 1974. *Changing schools: The magic feather principle.* New York: McGraw-Hill.

Berman, P. and McLaughlin, M.W. 1975. *Federal programs supporting educational change, vol. 7.* Santa Monica, CA: Rand Corporation.

Counts, G. S. 1932. *Dare the schools build a new social order?* New York: The John Day Co.

Fuller, F. F. and Bown, O. 1975. Becoming a teacher. In *Teacher education* (74th yearbook of the National Society for the Study of Education, Part II), ed. K. Ryan, 25–52. Chicago: University of Chicago Press.

Parker, F. W. 1897. My pedagogic creed I. *The School Journal* 53(8).

Percy, W. 1979. *The moviegoer.* New York: Alfred A. Knopf.

THE CONTRIBUTORS

Peter A. Barrett is Director of Studies for the Lower School at Saint Albans School in Washington, D.C. A doctoral candidate in education policy and planning at the University of Maryland, he is also the editor of *To Break the Silence: Thirteen Short Stories for Young Readers* and author of an accompanying teachers guide.

Shari Castle is Research and Development Coordinator for NEA's National Center for Innovation and systems operator for the IBM/NEA School Renewal Network. She is co-editor of *Teachers and Research in Action*.

Carlos E. Cortes is professor of history at the University of California, Riverside. Among his publications are *Three Perspectives on Ethnicity: Blacks, Chicanos, and Native Americans; Understanding You and Them; Gaucho Politics in Brazil; A Filmic Approach to the Study of Historical Dilemmas;* and *Images and Realities of Four World Regions.*

Arthur L. Costa is professor of education at California State University, Sacramento. He served as chair of the Department of Educational Administration for three years and currently teaches graduate courses to teachers and administrators in curriculum, supervision, and the improvement of instruction.

Gary A. Griffin is professor of education at the University of Arizona. He has conducted large-scale studies of teacher education, administered national research programs, served as Dean of Education at the University of Illinois at Chicago, and provided leadership as a teacher and administrator in public schools.

Madeleine R. Grumet is professor of education and Dean of the School of Education of Brooklyn College, City University of New York. Her book *Bitter Milk: Women and Teaching* (1989) is a study of the relation of our reproductive projects to epistemology, curriculum, and pedagogy.

Beverly Johnson is Coordinator for Research and Evaluation for NEA's National Center for Innovation. An elementary school teacher for 14 years, she has also worked with the University of Maryland's College of Education and its Center for Teaching and Learning; the Teacher Education Center in Montgomery County, Maryland; and the NEA Mastery In Learning Project.

Carol C. Livingston is assistant professor of education at The Catholic University of America. She is co-editor of *Teachers and Research in Action.*

Dorothy C. Massie, formerly the national editor of *Doubts & Certainties, Newsletter of the NEA Mastery In Learning Project,* wrote about many aspects of public education—principally school finance, personnel and human relations, school desegregation, and academic freedom—during her 23 years as an education writer and human relations specialist with NEA.

Terry Mazany is Director of Educational Initiatives for the National Center for Dispute Settlement in Southfield, Michigan. He has experience in the theory, design, and implementation of joint union-management programs in public-sector, private-sector, and educational settings and is currently directing the facilitation of Compact Schools for the Detroit Compact, a collaboration of the business community and the school system.

Robert M. McClure is Director of the NEA Mastery In Learning Consortium, National Center for Innovation. Long an advocate for curriculum reform and returning faculty to their rightful roles as key decision makers in schools, McClure has helped develop many of the Association's programs and publications on school improvement.

Lynne Miller is associate professor of administration and instructional leadership at the College of Education, University of Southern Maine. She also serves as the Executive Director of the Southern Maine Partnership, a school-university collaboration which is a member of John Goodlad's National Network for Educational Renewal.

Gary Rackliffe is associate professor in teacher education at Lake Superior State University, Sault Ste. Marie, Michigan. He works in the university's professional development school. His interests include the teacher's role in the life of the curriculum and how teachers use information to change their practice.

Marylyn Wentworth has been a teacher for 26 years and is now an educational consultant to public schools involved in change and restructuring, including work as the Mastery In Learning site consultant to Wells (Maine) Junior High School.